P9-BJY-971

Reaching People and Touching Lives Around the World

A Window of Opportunity for Global Outreach

Dr. Tracy Sharpe
and
Linda V. Sharpe

**Heart of Compassion
Missionary Ministries**

Copyright © 2009
by Dr. Tracy Sharpe and Linda V. Sharpe

Reaching People and Touching Lives
Around the World
A Window of Opportunity for Global Outreach
by Dr. Tracy Sharpe and Linda V. Sharpe

Printed in the United States of America

ISBN 978-1-60791-405-1

All rights reserved solely by the author. The author guarantees all contents are original and do not infringe upon the legal rights of any other person or work. No part of this book may be reproduced in any form without the permission of the author. The views expressed in this book are not necessarily those of the publisher.

Unless otherwise indicated, Bible quotations are taken from The King James Version of the Bible, Copyright © 1995 by the Zondervan Corporation and the Lockman Foundation, and The Amplified® Bible, AMP, Copyright © 1954, 1958, 1962, 1964, 1965, 1987 by The Lockman Foundation, and The Holy Bible, New International Version®, NIV®, Copyright © 1973, 1978, 1984 by International Bible Society, Used by permission of Zondervan, and The New King James Version, NKJV, Copyright © 1982 by Thomas Nelson, Inc., Used by Permission, and The *Holy Bible*, New Living Translation, NLT, Copyright © 1996 by Tyndale House Publishers, Inc., Wheaton, Illinois 60189, Used by permission, and *The Living Bible, TLB,* Copyright © 1971 by Tyndale House Publishers, Inc., Wheaton, Illinois 60189. Used by permission.

www.xulonpress.com

How then shall they call on him in whom they have not believed? and how shall they believe in him of whom they have not heard? and how shall they hear without a preacher? And how shall they preach, except they be sent?
—Romans 10:14–15

Contents

Acknowledgments

I would like to thank God for His inspiration in writing this book.

To my wife, Linda, you have been a blessing since I first met you in church. Your dedication toward missions helped to inspire me to what God has called me to do while living on this earth. I thank you for giving me a family. Finally, thank you for your input and support in writing this book.

To my two daughters, Kasi and Kaila, thank you for accepting me as your dad. To Kaila's husband, Marcus Dixon, God has a calling on your life. Seek Him first, and you will know your calling. To our new granddaughter, Layla, before you were ever born, God ordained you to serve Him.

To my mom and late father, Delores and Daniel Sharpe, thank you for your encouragement, from taking me to guitar lessons to teaching me right from wrong.

To Linda's mom and dad, Clara and Isaac Haynie, thank you for being an example for all Christians to follow.

To Sister Vera Boudreaux, your inspiration, service, and prayers are an encouragement for serving on the mission field.

To Bishop Joseph and Evangelist Bertha Wigfall, your continuous service of over fifty years serving on the mission field and supporting missionaries has resulted in many souls being saved around the world.

A warm thanks to all the faithful people who have donated their time and money to the vision that God has for Heart of Compassion Missionary Ministries.

Finally, to all of God's servants on the mission field, may God continue to provide for and protect you and your family.

Chapter 1

A Window of Opportunity

*And this gospel of the kingdom shall be
preached in all the world for a witness unto
all nations; and then shall the end come.*
— Matthew 24:14

More than ever before, we are hearing of wars
and rumors of wars; catastrophic natural
disasters; and devastating storms that are destroying
crops, wiping out livestock, and sending food prices
to record highs. In addition, some countries are
reporting cases of genocide, and others are facing
challenging economic conditions.

Despite the seriousness of these very real situations, however, such catastrophes have created
windows of opportunity for Christians to assist those
in need by giving their time while also sharing the
love of Christ. As believers, we must take advantage
of these opportunities through worldwide involve-

ment in providing humanitarian aid and economic assistance while simultaneously preaching the gospel.

During these times of worldwide turmoil, Christians who have a desire to serve as global witnesses for Christ can boldly step forward, knowing that God's commission to all believers is growing closer to fulfillment. But in order for the mandate to be realized, global-minded churches with leaders willing to work together must develop a strategic plan for conducting global outreach.

Although this book was not written to provide a detailed strategic plan for global evangelism, chapter 9, "Global Outreach," does include information that provides some basic concepts for preparing the Church to think globally before sending out a team of missionaries. This information can help to build a framework for the body of Christ to spread the gospel to all nations.

In Matthew 24:14, the Bible says, *"And this gospel of the kingdom shall be preached in all the world for a witness unto all nations; and then shall the end come."* We must continue to go into *all the world* and preach the gospel by whatever means necessary. Only God will know when this task has been completed; but when it has, the end shall come. Our task as Christians is to faithfully take the gospel to all nations.

Today Christians are entering nations that they previously had no opportunity to evangelize because of governmental restrictions (such restrictions are still the case in many countries throughout the world).

But as major disasters create global food shortages, Christians are becoming engaged in not only serving food for the stomachs of hungry people but also in providing spiritual food for dying souls. Despite these tremendous opportunities, however, challenges exist that must be faced before the gospel is preached throughout all the world.

Be Fruitful and Multiply

The Bible says in Genesis 1:27, *"So God created man in His own image; in the image of God He created him; male and female He created them"* (NKJV). God made man in His image; thus, man is the most important creation among all God's creations. Although sin separated man from God, God's desire from the beginning was for man to fill the earth and subdue it, using all its vast resources in the service of God and man.

In Genesis 9:7, the Bible says, *"And as for you, be fruitful and multiply; bring forth abundantly in the earth and multiply in it"* (NKJV). God first gave this command to Adam and then later to Noah. Since then, the world's population has increased phenomenally. At the time of this writing, based on data obtained from the U.S. Census Bureau, the world population is estimated to be more than 6.7 billion people.[1] Additionally, according to David Barrett, an expert on mission statistics and a contributing editor of the *World Christian Encyclopedia,* a breakdown of the estimated world population is as follows:

—One-third of the world's population consider themselves Christians.

—One-third are non-Christians living in reached people groups of the world.

—One-third are non-Christians living in unreached people groups of the world.[2]

In order to have a better understanding of this information, it is important to know what is meant by the term *people group*. A people group is defined as "a significantly large ethnic or sociological group of individuals who have a common similarity with one another."[3] In other words, it is a large group of people who have something in common that singles them out and identifies them as a separate group. That common factor might be language, religion, culture, location, or some other distinctive characteristic.

The term *unreached* refers to those people who have not yet heard the gospel. A combination of the two terms *unreached* and *people group* means an ethnic or social group that has not yet received any Christian witness or teaching. With this understanding of unreached people groups, the Church can target unreached areas of the world and develop a strategic global outreach plan to reach people groups who have yet to hear the gospel.

The information from the breakdown of the world's population exposes a couple of issues concerning the work that still must be done to spread the gospel. First, we must continue to reach out to non-Christians living in areas of the world where we have already made an effort through local evangelism. The Bible says, *"The Lord is not slack concerning his promise, as some count slackness, but is longsuffering toward us, not willing that any should perish but that all should come to repentance"* (2 Peter 3:9 NKJV). God loves us all and wants all people to know Him and have a personal relationship with Him. We must continue to preach the gospel and pray for those people who have had an opportunity but have not accepted Jesus as their Lord and Savior.

Second, the statistics reveal the necessity to focus on those unreached people groups who have not yet had an opportunity to know the Lord, which is why we must systematically direct our resources toward global outreach. By establishing a global outreach plan for reaching non-Christians in unreached areas of the world, Christians can pioneer a local church movement in areas where none exists. These unreached areas include over two billion people.

"For I have no pleasure in the death of one who dies," says the Lord God. "Therefore turn and live!" (Ezekiel 18:32 NKJV). God loves us and does not want any one of us to perish, so those who do not know Him must have an opportunity to hear the truth. This is why we must direct our efforts to give them a chance to call on Him, to believe in Him, and to hear Him through the Word of God preached by those whom He has called to go. We must, therefore, be wise with our resources and develop a global outreach strategy centered upon reaching the unreached people groups who do not yet know the Lord.

All Authority

The billions of unreached people in the world portray the unfinished task that Jesus has commissioned for all believers to accomplish. Scripture says, ***"And Jesus came and spoke to them, saying, 'All authority has been given to Me in heaven and on earth. Go therefore and make disciples of all the nations, baptizing them in the name of the Father and of the Son and of the Holy Spirit, teaching them to observe all things that I have commanded you; and lo, I am with you always, even to the end of the age' "*** (Matthew 28:18–20 NKJV).

As we look at this Scripture, the words *all authority* are important for believers to understand in order to fulfill what God has mandated in the remaining portion of the passage. The word *all* means "all" in Hebrew, Greek, Latin, Spanish, French, German, English, or Shona (a language spoken by many Zimbabweans). Jesus has given us *all* authority.

The next word, *authority,* as defined in *Merriam-Webster's Dictionary*, means "power to influence or command thought, opinion, or behavior." It also means "freedom granted by one in authority."[4] For example, in business, authority refers to the right to make decisions and to allocate resources in order to accomplish tasks that will achieve organizational goals. When managers delegate authority, they are able to complete their work assignments and achieve results without having to handle every task personally. Through Christ, God has delegated *all authority* to His people to accomplish His mission, and He expects each one of us to complete our assignments.

Business managers are delegated authority from their superiors; they are then evaluated based on the profits and losses of the corporation. In a similar fashion, God will judge us based on our obedience in accomplishing His mandate to take the gospel to all lands. This is why we must understand the authority that we have in Christ and use our God-given resources wisely in serving as witnesses for Christ.

Matthew 28:16–20, commonly known as the Great Commission, tells us what God's command is for His people, how to accomplish His purpose, and how to build His eternal kingdom. To fulfill this mission, we must learn to be disciples of Christ and grow spiritually so that we can carry out God's orders with all the authority and power He has delegated to us.

Spiritual Growth

Spiritual growth in the Word of God is necessary to effectively use the power and authority that God has given us. The Bible speaks about this in the book of Hebrews: *"You have been believers so long now that you ought to be teaching others. Instead, you need someone to teach you again the basic things about God's word. You are like babies who need milk and cannot eat solid food. For someone who lives on milk is still an infant and doesn't know how to do what is right. Solid food is for those who are mature, who through training have the skill to recognize the difference between right and wrong"* (Hebrews 5:12–14 NLT).

As we grow in the Word of God, we must not only learn how to lead people, but we must also develop the maturity to follow and receive correction from those who lead us. We must realize that God is no respecter of persons. In other words, God's dealings with us are not based on our outward appearance, age, position, rank, wealth, or nationality. God chooses whom He uses, and He deals with each one of us accordingly.

In 1 Samuel 2:26, the Bible says, *"Meanwhile, the boy Samuel grew taller and grew in favor with the LORD and with the people"* (NLT). While Samuel physically grew taller, he also grew in favor with the Lord. In other words, Samuel grew wiser in the things of God because he was devoted to God. Eli, the priest at that time, honored his sons above God, so God raised up an obedient and devoted believer, Samuel, to be His prophet. Samuel was chosen by God Himself, and all the people in the land knew that he was the Lord's prophet sent to teach the children of Israel.

Regardless of a person's age or position, God may choose to raise him or her up because of that person's willingness and obedience to follow His will, His way, and His commands. When we follow God with all our hearts, we will grow spiritually in favor with the Lord, just like Samuel did, and we position ourselves to be mightily used by Him.

David is another example of someone who grew in the Lord. In 2 Samuel 5:10, the Bible says, *"And*

*David went on, and grew great, and the L*ORD *God of hosts was with him."* At an early age, David grew in the Lord as he watched his flock of sheep. During the time when a lion and a bear attacked his father's flock, the Lord's presence was with him. The episode is recorded in 1 Samuel 17:34–35: *"And David said unto Saul, Thy servant kept his father's sheep, and there came a lion, and a bear, and took a lamb out of the flock: And I went out after him, and smote him, and delivered it out of his mouth: and when he arose against me, I caught him by his beard, and smote him, and slew him."* The Lord gave His Spirit to David, a man after His own heart, so that David might lead Israel with God's help, direction, and blessing (1 Samuel 13:14; 16:6–15). As a young man, David matured and learned to seek and trust God. He grew to know God and had confidence in the Lord's presence in life and death, in righteousness and weakness, in comfort and in distress. Psalm 23 beautifully expresses David's trust in God and his understanding of being led by the Good Shepherd.

Over a period of time, David learned not only how to be led by God but also how to lead people and receive correction from his leaders when he made mistakes. Throughout his life, both as a boy and later as king, David came to know God as he grew and matured spiritually, and we must do the same.

Giving and receiving instruction is not something new for any of us, but it does require that we grow spiritually and mature in Christ. In 1 Corinthians 13:11, the Bibles says, *"When I was a child, I spoke as a child, I understood as a child, I thought as a child; but when I became a man, I put away childish things"* (NKJV). As children, we receive instruction from our parents, our teachers, and from those who care for us. As we grow into adulthood, we find ourselves becoming parents, grandparents, employees, or even supervisors on the job, many times without much advance preparation. It's almost as though it happens automatically, with little or no thought on our part.

Growing in the Lord, however, is not automatic. It happens only when we purpose for it to happen and only as we read God's Word and pray. But as we grow spiritually in Christ, we can confidently and effectively use the authority and power that He has given to us. We must, therefore, purposefully put away childish things and feed on the Word of God if we expect to grow in the Lord.

The Bible says, *"Like newborn babies, you must crave pure spiritual milk so that you will grow into a full experience of salvation. Cry out for this nour-ishment, now that you have had a taste of the Lord's kindness"* (1 Peter 2:2–3 NLT). Milk is an essential part of a baby's diet. Without milk, the baby will die. When we are born again into the family of God, we become babes in Christ. Without our spiritual milk, the Word of God, we too will die.

Whether we are new Christians or mature ones, our spiritual growth depends on how much time we spend praying and reading God's Word. Once we have matured to a certain point, however, we no longer feed as children, but as adults. That means we are capable of taking in larger amounts and digesting it more efficiently. We can tolerate meat rather than just milk. Mature Christians voraciously devour the Word daily, just as a hungry lion feeds daily on its prey. This causes them to continue to mature in Christ and to exercise their authority to boldly go forth preaching the gospel.

Discipline and Obedience

We must also recognize that sometimes we need help in the area of disciplining ourselves so that we can grow spiritually in the Lord. I learned the importance of discipline while serving as an officer in the United States Army. During this time, I learned to both receive and give orders. Sometimes my orders were specific, and other times they were general, depending on the situation. But the key characteristics of both receiving and giving orders were the same: discipline and obedience.

My time in the military helped me to mature and become disciplined in my life, and this carried over into my personal walk with Christ. As Christians, and regardless of our circumstances, we all must learn to be obedient followers and disciplined leaders by executing the orders that God gives us. We all must continue to grow in the Lord, as Samuel and David did, and use the authority that Christ has given us to serve as witnesses unto all nations.

We Must Go

As we grow spiritually in the Lord and recognize our God-given authority, we can begin to effectively carry out God's orders. Jesus has given all believers specific orders, stated in Matthew 28:16–20: to "go," to go and "make disciples," and to go and make disciples of "all nations." Let's look at the first command: to go.

The word *go,* according to *Merriam-Webster's Dictionary,* means "to move on a course or to proceed without delay."[5] As Christians, we have been commanded to go. We must move on the course that God has directed and proceed without delay, because we do not know the day or the hour that the Son of Man will return. Scripture illustrates this point clearly: *"It's like a man going away: He leaves his house and puts his servants in charge, each with his assigned task, and tells the one at the door to keep watch. Therefore keep watch because you do not know when the owner of the house will come back—whether in the evening, or at midnight, or when the rooster crows, or at dawn. If he comes suddenly, do not let him find you sleeping. What I say to you, I say to everyone: 'Watch!' "* (Mark 13:34–37 NIV).

We must be thorough in completing our task of spreading the gospel to all people. Jesus came to save the lost, regardless of their circumstances, situations, ethnic backgrounds, or ways of life. Whether someone is a follower of Islam, Hinduism, or Buddhism, or is a follower of tribal worship, *"the Son of Man has come to seek and save that which was lost"* (Luke 19:10 NKJV). People no longer have to go through life not knowing where they will go when they die; as long as they are willing to accept Jesus as their Lord and Savior, they are included in those whom He came to save.

Jesus diligently sought the lost. He sought them in people's homes; in fields; in and under trees; on boats; by the sea; in the temple; by wells; on the Mount of Olives; on mountaintops; in valleys; and throughout many geographical regions, such as Judea, Galilee, Jerusalem, Samaria, Jordan, and Capernaum. As believers, we must follow this example of actively seeking the lost. That means we must "go" to the grocery store, to the school, to the park, to the job, and to the shopping center. We must "go" to places like Ethiopia, Morocco, Haiti, Algeria, Zimbabwe, Chad, Cote d'Ivoire, China, North Korea, and every other place where God has called Christians to serve as His witnesses.

My wife, Linda, and I have made seeking the lost our calling. One place where we have done this is at Hopley Farm, a squatters' camp located on the outskirts of Harare, Zimbabwe. Composed of approximately seven thousand displaced residents, Hopley Farm is home to thousands of people who were forced out of another camp and required to move to Hopley Farm in 2004 and 2005.

As of October 2008, this camp still had no infrastructure or adequate housing. The people live in makeshift huts and do not have adequate safe water or sanitation. Also, as a result of Zimbabwe's rotting infrastructure, cholera is spreading rapidly because untreated sewage is infecting the drinking water. Additionally, the lack of proper drainage, coupled with the frequent rains, provides the perfect breeding place for mosquitoes, which ultimately leads to more cases of malaria. It's also sad because elderly people, pregnant women, people with HIV and AIDS, and countless children must spend their nights huddled in the overcrowded shelters in an attempt to avoid the rain. Unfortunately, this very unhealthy situation is apt to have a long-term negative effect on the community.

As we have ministered to the people at Hopley Farm, Linda and I have pledged to help them by building the first church in that area. Knowing that the call to go is all-inclusive, we are spurred into action in even the most desperate, forgotten places on earth, places like Hopley Farm.

Acts 1:8 presents a challenge for all believers to go and serve as witnesses for Christ everywhere: in the community (Jerusalem), throughout the state (Judea), on another continent (Samaria), and to the world (the ends of the earth). Christians must heed this mandate and the example that has been presented and go as Jesus commanded. Although not every believer is called to go to another nation, all believers can participate in spreading the gospel by giving "provision for the vision" to those who have been called to go to other lands.

Make Disciples

As we go to other nations, God has also commanded us to make disciples of those whom we reach. The word *disciple* literally means "learner," so a disciple of Christ is not only a believer but also a learner in the things of God.

Disciples are imitators of their teachers, because the goal of a disciple is to be like his master. This is clear in the Scriptures: ***"Therefore be imitators of God [copy Him and follow His example], as well-beloved children [imitate their father]"*** (Ephesians 5:1 AMP).

As believers, we must strive to be like our master, Jesus Christ. We must pattern our lives after His so that our love will be visible to the world. We must show the world that we are not just casual church attendees, but committed church members who are true followers of Christ.

True disciples are committed to the teachings of Christ and possess a genuine love for people. Their hearts are filled with the desire to lead others to the Lord. In other words, because they are disciples of Jesus, they reproduce themselves in others and thus advance the kingdom of God.

All Nations

Matthew 28:16–20 also instructs believers to make disciples of all nations. There is already at least one church in every political nation of the world, so does this mean that we've already reached all the nations? No, it most certainly does not! God's view of nations and our view of nations are two completely different things.

Before attempting to make disciples of all nations, we must have a better understanding of the word *nations* as stated in this passage. After a thorough study of this Scripture, I learned that many Christians misunderstand this. Many believers see the word *nations* in Matthew 28:19 and incorrectly assume that it refers to political nations or individual countries.

However, the word translated "nations" comes from the Greek word *ethnos*. We get the English word *ethnic* from *ethnos,* but the word is translated in the Scripture as "nations." More correctly, this word means peoples, people groups, or tribes, rather than countries. Also, in the biblical context, the word *nations* is more properly defined by language, culture, and geographical location. So when we put the translation of the word *nations* in perspective with the rest of the Scripture, we see that believers must go and make disciplined followers of Christ in all ethnicities, or people groups.

With this more precise knowledge and understanding, the Church can develop a new vision in global evangelism by focusing on people groups rather than on nations or individual countries. Without this understanding, it is easy to misinterpret our mission and to believe that since we have been to every nation or country, we have already completed the Great Commission.

When the proper interpretation of the word *nations* is understood, however, we easily recognize that our mission is far from complete. In fact, the mission is so far-reaching that it requires a united effort on the part of all churches, mission agencies, and research organizations to learn where to focus efforts and obtain data concerning unreached ethnic or people groups of the world.

One research organization that provides data concerning unreached people groups is the Joshua Project. The Joshua Project obtains data from mission agencies, local and international researchers, church planters, local churches, individuals, and missionaries to develop a list of all ethnic peoples around the world. This research organization also tracks data concerning reached and unreached ethnic or people groups and defines terms that can help church leaders unite in establishing a strategy for global outreach. The data obtained from the Joshua Project provides another tool for reaching the unreached people groups around the world by creating a window of opportunity for global-minded leaders and churches to conduct global evangelism.

Even though a shifting in thought must take place in the body of Christ, the mandate is still clear. Now is the time to execute His orders by going into areas where the gospel has not been preached and where people are in dire need of help. The task may seem daunting, but the Bible says, *"With God nothing shall be impossible"* (Luke 1:37). God has given His Church everything needed to do as He commanded. Now is the time to go, because now there is a window of opportunity to reach people and touch lives around the world.

Chapter 2

A Paradigm Shift

*And be not conformed to this world: but be
ye transformed by the renewing of your mind,
that ye may prove what is that good, and
acceptable, and perfect, will of God.*
— Romans 12:2

The mandate to go, as stated in the Great
Commission, should compel church leaders
to use their resources to develop a strategic global
outreach plan to reach lost souls. Unfortunately, many
church organizations are not using the available data,
or they are unaware of the information that can help
them channel their resources for global outreach. In
any case, before change can take place in the church
and before the body of Christ can effectively reach
out globally, there must be a spiritual paradigm shift,
or a transformation in the way that believers approach
global evangelism.

By now, I am sure that you're asking, "What's a spiritual paradigm shift?" Let's begin by defining the word *paradigm.* According to the *World English Dictionary,* a paradigm is "an example that serves as a pattern or model."[6] It refers to the framework by which we live our lives and perceive things. When something occurs that totally changes the pattern, model, or perspective in the way that we view certain things, we say a paradigm shift has occurred. For example, people once believed that the earth was flat. When people began to realize that the earth was actually a sphere, a revolutionary new perspective emerged. This new perspective resulted in a paradigm shift concerning the way people viewed the shape of the earth.

In another example, people now obtain information by using the Internet more than by reading newspapers. Although there is nothing wrong with receiving news and information from the newspaper, the Internet is the new model and has changed our fundamental view of how we receive information. This is a paradigm shift from how we once received news and information to how we now receive it via the Internet.

A paradigm shift is powerful, and based on the influence of just one individual; it can even change a society. Many examples in history exist—both positive and negative—where one person led a small group, which led to a movement, which ultimately led to an entire population shifting its paradigm from one way of thinking to something totally different. You might think that it's impossible for a person to steer an entire population, but it's true. It has happened before, and it can happen again.

Although there is nothing wrong with change, we must be prayerful that the change represents a shift in the direction that God intended. For example, Martin Luther King Jr. led a large segment of the population *from believing* that separate but equal was right *to believing* the biblically correct paradigm that God created all people in His image. By contrast, Adolf Hitler led a nation into believing that Jews were taking over the world and needed to be eliminated, thus adversely shifting people's beliefs and thoughts about an entire race of people. It took a world war and millions of deaths before Hitler and his anti-Semitic paradigm were finally defeated. The point is, it is possible for one person to change a group's thinking, for a group to change the thinking of a number of groups, and for an entire nation to make a radical paradigm shift.

In the spiritual realm, a paradigm shift means a spiritual change in how a believer thinks that *affects* or *infects* the direction of many members in the body of Christ. Jim Jones is a prime example of someone who shifted people away from the Bible to his own ungodly view, or paradigm. As a result, over nine hundred members of the People's Temple committed suicide in Jonestown, Guyana, in November 1978. This is, of course, an extreme case, but a spiritual paradigm shift can happen subtly over a period of time. The Bible warns us to watch out for this: ***"Behold, I send you out as sheep in the midst of wolves. Therefore be wise as serpents and harmless*** *as doves"* (Matthew 10:16 NKJV). We must be wise and watchful of the adversary as the end times draw nearer and worldwide turmoil subtly shifts our priorities away from God and global evangelism.

Even today a spiritual paradigm shift is subtly turning the focus of the body of Christ away from God's mandate. The Bible says, *"For we wrestle not against flesh and blood, but against principalities, against powers, against the rulers of the darkness of this world, against spiritual wickedness in high places"* (Ephesians 6:12). We cannot forget that there are evil spiritual forces fighting to shift our beliefs and focus from what God mandated, the reaching of lost souls, to focusing on our own situations.

But over two thousand years ago, God gave the body of Christ a mandate to reach the lost, and that mandate has not changed. Nevertheless, a subtle shift is preventing many believers from moving forward to fulfill it. Churches are spending more time on church growth conferences, praise and worship conferences, leadership conferences, financial conferences, pastors' conferences, women's conferences, and men's conferences than in reaching lost souls. There is nothing wrong with having conferences, but when conferences rather than lost souls become the priority, we need to recognize that the adversary is subtly shifting the body of Christ into a paradigm away from God's mandate.

The Word of God never changes. The command to go into the world to preach the gospel is still the same; this is why the body of Christ must be watchful not to allow life's circumstances to alter its spiritual paradigm. The Bible clearly tells us, *"And be not conformed to this world: but be ye transformed by the renewing of your mind, that ye may prove what is that good, and acceptable, and perfect, will of God"* (Romans 12:2). God's perfect will is for *all* people to worship Him in *all* of His glory. For God to use us to accomplish His perfect will, we must renew our minds and shift our thinking in the way we view nations, people groups, and global outreach. Again, the mandate to go into the world and preach the gospel has not changed; people and their circumstances change, but the paradigm does not.

A subtle paradigm shift away from global outreach can result in a shift away from reaching lost souls. We must be careful not to allow conferences or even small activities meant to edify and direct the body of Christ to steer us away from God's mandate. James 3:4–5 helps us to understand this. The verse says, *"Look also at ships: although they are so large and are driven by fierce winds, they are turned by a very small rudder wherever the pilot desires. Even so the tongue is a little member and boasts great things"* (NKJV). The rudder on a ship is a small part, but based on the actions of the captain the direction of the entire ship can change. As Christians, we also control our direction by our actions in the same manner that a captain controls the direction of a ship. We must be careful not to become preoccupied with conferences and other activities that the adversary can use to subtly shift the body of Christ away from God's mandate of reaching out globally for lost souls. We must stay on course and as Paul stated in his letter to the Philippians, we must *"press toward the mark for the prize of the high calling of God in Christ Jesus"* (Philippians 3:14).

Prayer Changes People

Only a radical paradigm shift will enable believers to let go of how they see the world and embrace how God sees it and what He expects of His people. It may call for a shift from being locally minded to becoming globally minded and reallocating resources to be more in line with God's global purpose. Such change, however, will not happen by accident; rather, it will happen only through prayer, meditating in the Word, and fasting. But once that change has taken place in the hearts and minds of believers, a spiritual paradigm shift will occur in the body of Christ and ultimately transform the way we think about global outreach.

Many countries today are experiencing political turmoil and the resulting economic instability that often accompanies it, but no change will occur until a spiritual paradigm shift takes place in the hearts and minds of the people. My wife and I serve on the mission field in Zimbabwe, and as much as we long for change, we realize that a spiritual shift must occur before the political and economic situation can change in this country. Church leaders must come together in an outward demonstration of prayer, much like Paul and Silas did when thrown into prison for doing the work of the gospel. As these two powerful church leaders united through prayer and praise unto God, prison doors opened and everyone's shackles were loosed. That is the kind of prayer that changes nations, and that is the kind of prayer we need today.

Many people fervently desire and even expect change, but the obstacles of famine, poverty, and injustice will never be overcome through desire alone. As James 5:16 says, *"The effectual fervent prayer of a righteous man availeth much."* Church leaders and believers must set their egos aside and unite in prayer to facilitate real change in the political and economic landscapes in their countries.

The Bible furnishes many examples of people who experienced paradigm shifts in order to do the will of God. Genesis 12:1 records, *"Now the Lord had said to Abram: Get out of your country, from your family and from your father's house, to a land that I will show you"* (NKJV). This Scripture shows the paradigm shift that had to take place in Abram's life to change his thinking from something familiar and comfortable to something unfamiliar and probably uncomfortable. At the age of seventy-five, Abram moved from his country and from his relative's house to a new land that he knew nothing about. Abram radically altered his lifestyle, even though he was already blessed with material possessions and servants. But Abram, regardless of the cost or inconvenience, shifted his paradigm in order to do God's will.

Another example is found in 1 Samuel 8:5–7. This passage illustrates a paradigm shift that resulted from circumstances different from Abram's, but it was a paradigm shift nonetheless. In these verses, the people of Israel rejected God's servant Samuel as judge and asked for a king over Israel. God granted their request, even though the people had shifted to a spiritual direction not in accordance with His original plan. As we read the Bible, however, we see that God's plan never changes. Whether it takes one year or a thousand years, God's plan eventually comes to pass. In the case of Israel, another paradigm shift occurred many years later when the people's desire to have a king as ruler was changed to God's plan of having the King of kings as ruler over all humanity!

The Eyes of Christ

A paradigm shift will occur in the lives of believers when they begin to see themselves as God sees them. God sees Christians as accepted and complete in Christ: *"But to all who believed him and accepted him, he gave the right to become children of God"* (John 1:12 NLT). Furthermore, *"For in Christ lives all the fullness of God in a human body. So you also are complete through your union with Christ, who is the head over every ruler and authority"* (Colossians 2:9–10 NLT).

The love that a parent has for a child is but a tiny glimpse of God's love for us. When we become believers, we are adopted into His family, and He accepts us as His very own. Everything that belongs to God now belongs to us because we are joint heirs with Christ. He adopts us as members of His body and unites us with Him in spirit. In fact, we are complete in Him; and because of Him, we have direct access to the throne of grace. As Christians, we must see ourselves in the same manner that God sees us.

God also sees us as secure and significant in Christ: *"And we know that all things work together for good to those who love God, to those who are the called according to His purpose"* (Romans 8:28 NKJV). *"For we are His workmanship, created in Christ Jesus for good works, which God prepared beforehand that we should walk in them"* (Ephesians 2:10 NKJV).

Because we are significant to God, we have security and freedom from any condemnation brought against us. Furthermore, He will never give up on us, no matter what we do. This was exemplified by the action of His Son, Jesus, in dying for us. If God paid the ultimate sacrifice of giving up his Son for us, I am sure that He won't give up on us and will never change His mind about it. In fact, God loved us even while we were sinners.

As we realize how God sees us and how important all people are to Him, we will be motivated to make every effort to go to the unreached areas of the world. There are over two billion people living in unreached areas who have not yet had the opportunity to experience God's acceptance, completeness, security, and significance.

Shifting Priorities

Understanding who we are in Christ helps us to develop a mind like Christ's, and God's mandate will then become our priority. But until this happens, the global mission will remain unfulfilled, and the finances needed for it will be used for other purposes. For the Church to have the finances to send people into the world, there must first be a paradigm shift in how money is spent within the body of Christ. Unfortunately, in many cases, this paradigm shift has not yet occurred. Church leaders have opted to increase funding for local church programs, building projects, conferences, and local outreach but have neglected to fund the requirements needed for global outreach. This is a sad reality.

A spiritual paradigm shift that moves believers from one way of thinking (locally) to another (globally) is necessary for change to take place in the church. This can come about only through a transformation of the minds and hearts of believers. As we grow in Christ, we will stagnate at one level of spiritual development and never mature into the people God intended us to be unless we are willing to embrace new paradigms. But God will help us and create situations that allow our paradigms to shift in order to bring us out of the past and the future and into the "right now." Faith is *now,* and we must believe that whatever we ask for in prayer will happen *now.*

As we begin to understand who we are in Christ and conform to God's Word, our thinking will be transformed to God's way of doing things. The Bible declares, *"Jesus Christ the same yesterday, and today, and for ever"* (Hebrews 13:8). God's Word is a firm and immovable foundation containing principles that never change. We must do what God originally called us to do in His Word, even though that may require a shift in our thinking or a shake-up in the way that we operate and view global outreach. Then, as we continue to do those activities in line with God's mandate, we will discover that *"those things which cannot be shaken [will] remain"* (Hebrews 12:27).

All Things Are Possible

With the authority that we have in Christ and the power given to us through the Holy Spirit, God will draw people to us so that He can use us to lead unbelievers to repentance. Through our prayers, the Holy Spirit will transform the hearts of those who do not know Christ and make them new creations (2 Corinthians 5:17). God has chosen to give us the responsibility of sharing His message of salvation, redemption, forgiveness, and truth, but we must be obedient. The Bible says, *"As You sent Me into the world, I have sent them into the world"* (John 17:18 NKJV). If church leaders will balance the priorities of the church by helping people in their communities while at the same time releasing the needed resources toward global outreach, God's vision for the people of this earth will be accomplished: *"For the earth shall be filled with the knowledge of the glory of the LORD, as the waters cover the sea"* (Hebrews 2:14).

A paradigm shift might seem new, different, or even extreme, but we must take advantage of this window of opportunity that God has opened. We must look toward God, rather than the immensity of the task. We must pray that God's desire, *"that none should perish,"* would become a priority for all Christians. We must also pray that His desire will ignite a spiritual paradigm shift in the body of Christ toward global evangelism. Finally, we must pray that God will send people to give provision for the vision and that He will send more laborers to complete the mission.

Chapter 3

Reaching People and Touching Lives Around The World

"For from the rising of the sun, even to its going down, My name shall be great among the Gentiles; in every place incense shall be offered to My name, and a pure offering; for My name shall be great among the nations," says the LORD of hosts.

—Malachi 1:11 NKJV

The 10/40 Window

The time is coming when people of all nations will worship the greatness of God. But it will take more than the efforts of church leaders to reach the unreached; it will take the entire body of Christ globally uniting to spread the gospel in restricted and hostile areas of the world.

One such area where a vast majority of unreached people live is the region known as the 10/40 Window. The area gets its name based on its location, which is between 10 and 40 degrees north latitude of the Equator. The 10/40 Window, stretching from North Africa to the Middle East to Asia to the Far East, includes two-thirds of the world's population but accounts for only one-third of the earth's total land area.

My wife and I refer to this area as the 10/40 "Window of Opportunity," because a unique window of opportunity exists there to reach unreached people. Home to the majority of the world's unevangelized countries, the 10/40 Window has the largest population of non-Christians who have not heard the gospel.

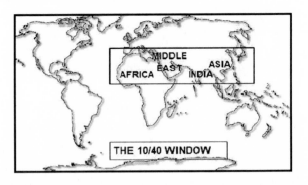

We Christians have the power and authority to break all the spiritual strongholds of Satan and every demonic spirit in the 10/40 Window, but we must exercise our authority through prayer and fasting, and we must also take action by developing a strategic global outreach plan to win lost souls. As we do this, we must trust God's Word: *"A man's heart plans his way, but the LORD directs his steps"* (Proverbs 16:9 NKJV). God will direct our steps, but we must do our part by planning. As we plan our way, we must also consider the vast resources available to help us develop an effective plan for global outreach.

For example, the U.S. Center for World Mission and the Joshua Project initiative provide much data to assist in developing a strategic global outreach plan. These organizations supply statistics on the number of people groups in an area, their religious beliefs, languages spoken, country profiles, and other useful statistical information. This information can be used to help church leaders, pastors, missionaries, and anyone interested in global outreach focus on specific people groups in a country of interest, thereby effectively reaching the billions of unreached souls around the world.

A Historical and Biblical Significance

Upon reviewing some of the data obtained through the Joshua Project, it becomes evident that there are many countries with historical and biblical significance located in the heart of the 10/40 Window. The biblical account of Adam and Eve's creation and God's plan for them to have dominion in the earth as stated in Genesis 1:26 occurred within the 10/40 Window. Additionally, Adam and Eve's sin that caused them to lose their right to rule the earth, the account of the flood, and the building of the Tower of Babel, which led to God's scattering of the people and the formation of people groups, occurred in the 10/40 Window.

Additional information from the Joshua Project reveals an estimated 6,700 unreached people groups living in the 10/40 Window, accounting for more than two billion souls who have not heard the gospel. Furthermore, the overwhelming majority of the world's least evangelized megacities are in the 10/40 Window (megacities are those cities with a population of more than one million people).

Because of the historical and biblical significance of the 10/40 Window, coupled with the vast number of people living there who have not had the opportunity to hear the gospel, this area is ideal for strategic global plans to reach the unreached peoples of the world.

The Religious Strongholds

Knowing and understanding the religious strongholds in the 10/40 Window is another aspect of this region that Christians must consider when planning global outreaches. Four religious blocs dominate the 10/40 Window, and their strongholds must be broken before Christians can obtain a foothold in this region of nonbelievers. These four religious blocs include Islam, Hinduism, Buddhism, and nonreligious sects. These groups have made preaching the gospel a challenge for Christians because of the existing spiritual strongholds and fanatical beliefs that are a major characteristic of many of their followers. An overview of these religions is listed below to provide Christians with a basic understanding of their differing views and beliefs and to help in planning global outreaches throughout the world.

Islam — Islam is a monotheistic religion, meaning its followers believe in one God. Islam is based on the teachings of Muhammad, a seventh-century Arab religious and political figure. In Arabic, the word *Islam* means "submission" (to Allah). A follower of Islam is called a Muslim or Moslem, a term which means "one who submits" (to God). Muslims follow the teachings of Muhammad, whom they regard as God's last and greatest prophet.

Hinduism — Hinduism is the fourth largest religion in the world and is the oldest among all major religions. Historians believe that Hinduism originated more than five thousand years ago. It is sometimes called "the religion of India," because approximately 800 million of the world's 1 billion Hindus live in India and about 80 percent of Indians are Hindus. Hindus believe in reincarnation and eventual unity with what is known as Brahman, as well as respect for all life forms. The goal of Hindus is to follow four lifelong aims: righteousness, material success, love and pleasure, and release from reincarnation and thus reunification with Brahman.

Buddhism — Buddhism is classified as the fifth largest religion in the world. It is a belief system that teaches that desire causes suffering; thus, if desire is eliminated, enlightenment and nirvana can be attained. Much of modern Buddhism is either atheistic, which means rejecting any belief in any gods, or agnostic, which refers to one who is not committed to believing in either the existence or the nonexistence of God or a god. The term *Buddha* means "the enlightened one."

Nonreligious — Nonreligious beliefs refer to a set of beliefs or religions that are ethnic or tribal in nature. Each group has its own particular tradition and belief.

The map illustration provided below depicts the four religious blocs in the 10/40 Window. As you look at the map, you will notice that Muslims are prominent in the western part of the 10/40 Window, which stretches across the north of Africa into the Middle East. In the south, Asia is in the middle of the 10/40 Window and is the heart of Hinduism, which acknowledges over 330 million gods. Buddhism, the primary religion in Southeast Asia, prevails in the eastern part of the 10/40 Window. The nonreligious areas make up the remainder of the four religious blocs in the 10/40 Window.

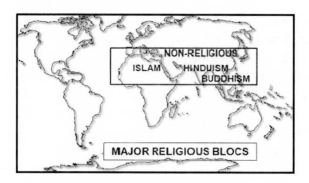

The four religious blocs in the 10/40 Window represent over four billion people, of which more than two billion have yet to hear the gospel. The difficulties facing many missionaries who go to these countries stem mainly from the political and fanatical religious beliefs of people who live in these religious blocs, thus creating major challenges to get an opportunity to preach the gospel. For example, in some countries, preaching the gospel or converting to Christianity is a crime punishable by death.

Additionally, we must also consider the social, cultural, and geographical barriers that hinder the spreading of the gospel. This is why we must learn more about the different religions and people of the 10/40 Window if we hope to break the spiritual strongholds throughout this region.

The Poor and Lost

Another fact that global evangelists must consider is that the 10/40 Window is home to the majority of the world's poor. The Bible says *"Blessed is he who considers the poor; The LORD will deliver him in time of trouble. The LORD will preserve him and keep him alive, And he will be blessed on the earth; You will not deliver him to the will of his enemies. The LORD will strengthen him on his bed of illness; You will sustain him on his sickbed"* (Psalm 41:1-3 NKJV). Of the poorest of the poor, more than eight out of ten live in the 10/40 Window. On the average, they exist on less than a few hundred dollars per person per year, according to information obtained from the Joshua Project. Brent L. Myers, in his article entitled "Where Are the Poor and Lost?" states that "the poor are the lost, and the lost are the poor."[7] Myers drew this conclusion after discovering that the majority of the unreached live in the poorest countries of the world.

Because of this overlap between the poorest countries of the world and those that are least evangelized, we must make a concerted effort to reach the poor. Like us, they are God's people. Jesus died for everybody: the rich, the poor, and everyone in between. The poor have names, gifts, and talents, and God can use them just like He does with people who do not live in poverty. Thus any global outreach plan must take into consideration the specific needs of an area, especially in areas with a large number of poor people.

Strategize and Unite

Finally, the spiritual strongholds dominating the billions of people living in the 10/40 Window have not only caused poverty and disease of the area, but they have also kept the multitudes from the power of the gospel. Many people in this area have been blinded by the god of this world: *"The god of this age has blinded the minds of unbelievers, so that they cannot see the light of the gospel of the glory of Christ, who is the image of God"* (2 Corinthians 4:4 NIV).

For a spiritual paradigm shift to take place, the Church must use the information provided by the Joshua Project and other organizations to gain insight on how to effectively strategize and plan global missions throughout the 10/40 Window. Then, even though the challenges are great, we must go and fulfill the scriptural mandate. When we do, *"the whole earth will acknowledge the LORD and return to him. All the families of the nations will bow down before him"* (Psalm 22:27 NLT).

There will come a day when everyone will have had an opportunity to hear the gospel. But to successfully reach people and touch lives around the world, believers in the body of Christ must unite in prayer, missionaries must go, people must fund the mission, and Christians must overcome the internal challenges facing many churches and the inherent conditions already existing in the countries of the 10/40 Window.

In the book of Revelation, the apostle John writes, *"After these things I looked, and behold, a great multitude which no one could number, of all nations, tribes, peoples, and tongues, standing before the throne and before the Lamb, clothed with white robes, with palm branches in their hands, and crying out with a loud voice, saying, 'Salvation belongs to our God who sits on the throne, and to the Lamb!' "* (Revelation 7:9 NKJV). The great multitude in heaven will include all the faithful believers from every land and people group who remained faithful to God throughout the generations, *"for many are called, but few are chosen"* (Matthew 22:14). It is our job to extend the invitation to the uttermost corners of the earth.

Chapter 4

God Chooses Whom He Uses

You did not choose Me, but I chose you and appointed you that you should go and bear fruit, and that your fruit should remain, that whatever you ask the Father in My name He may give you.

—John 15:16 NKJV

We can all find reasons why God shouldn't have chosen us, but we could also wonder the same thing about people in the Bible whom God did choose. We could say that David was too young and Abraham too old for God to use. Gideon and Thomas both doubted God. Jonah ran from God, and David had an affair. Moses was stressed out, and Peter denied the Lord.

But when God looks at us, He doesn't see our sins. God sees us sinless because of the sacrifice of His Son. When we love and hunger for God, He will use us—in spite of who we are, where we have been, or what we look like. There are many reasons why God shouldn't have chosen us, but *God chooses whom He uses*. It is not man who does the choosing, but God.

Sometimes society or our family members try to choose for us. In India many people live under a caste system in which their spouses, occupations, and social status have already been chosen, based on heredity. Even in Western societies, some families, even though with good intentions, plan the lives of their children. For example, a family may own a farm, a professional business, or even a local grocery store in which the children are expected to work once they come of age. In another situation, families may push hard to get their children into a prestigious college or university and then expect them to go to work for a large corporation. But regardless of the country we grow up in, the caste that society places us in, or even the job or college that our family chooses for us, God has the final decision where we will end up, because *God chooses whom He uses*. Not society, not the caste system, and not our family members, but God Himself chooses our destiny.

Spiritual Fruit

When God chooses us, we are expected to go and bear fruit. This fruit is not the fruit that we pick and then eat, but it is the fruit of the Spirit, which represents visible growth in Jesus Christ. The fruit of the Spirit represents nine visible attributes of Christian living. These attributes are listed in Galatians 5:22–23: *"love, joy, peace, longsuffering, gentleness, goodness, faith, meekness, temperance."*

The fruit of the Spirit characterizes the lives of all who truly walk in the Spirit. If we are disciples of Christ, people should be able to see fruit in our lives. Jesus said, *"When you produce much fruit, you are my true disciples. This brings great glory to my Father"* (John 15:8 NLT). Jesus also said, *"By their fruits you will know them"* (Matthew 7:20 NKJV). We must remain loyal to God and be more concerned with God's glory and honor than with our own. When we do this, we will bring forth good fruit.

The Bible says that God's chosen and appointed children *"should go and bear fruit and this fruit should remain"* (John 15:16 NKJV). In particular, one of the fruits mentioned in Galatians 5:22 is very important, and that is the fruit of love. The Bible is not referring to the love that represents emotional affections, but to the love that characterizes willing and self-sacrificial service. God chose and appointed us to demonstrate our love to and for people, as He has demonstrated His love for the world.

In John 3:16, the Bible says, *"For God so loved the world, that he gave his only begotten Son, that whosoever believeth in him should not perish, but have everlasting life."* God's love for us was demonstrated through His Son, Jesus, who bore the sins of all humanity on the cross. When we accept Jesus as our Lord and Savior, we receive the eternal love of Christ that will not perish but will be everlasting life for those who believe. Through Christ, that same eternal love is available to all the unreached people groups of the world who have yet to hear the gospel.

All Christians have been chosen by the true and living God to go into the world to offer the fruit of love that comes through the Spirit of Christ to all who are willing to receive Jesus as Lord and Savior. When God chooses us, we are not limited by society, a caste system, or by family members, because God has chosen us to do greater works far above that which we could ever think or imagine.

God Chooses—Not Man

God chose Abram (later renamed Abraham in Genesis 17:5). He called one man and his family, and through them God blessed all the families of the earth. He called him to a land that he had never seen (Genesis 12:1), and Abram left his home and his country because he trusted and believed God. Because of Abram's obedience and commitment to God, God promised him three things: land, a great nation through his descendants, and a blessing that would affect all the nations of the earth (Genesis 12:2–3). When we are obedient and committed to God, He can use us to be a blessing to others, just like He did with Abraham, because *God chooses whom He uses.*

God chose Samuel when he was just a child, but he was obviously old enough to work, because the Bible says that he *"opened the doors of the house of the Lord"* (1 Samuel 3:15). God chose to work through Samuel to bring the final message of judgment to Eli. After Samuel received the message from the Lord concerning Eli, the Bible says, *"Samuel lay down until morning. . . . And Samuel was afraid to tell Eli the vision"* (1 Samuel 3:15 NKJV). Under Eli's questioning, however, Samuel revealed everything that the Lord had told him. Eli submitted to the message of judgment from the Lord, but he still did nothing to stop his two sons' immoral sins.

God chose Samuel to proclaim His word, even though Samuel was just a young child. Whatever our position in society, whether we are an adult or a child, *God chooses whom He uses.*

Another example of God's sovereign choice is found in the book of Jeremiah: *"Before I formed you in the womb I knew you, before you were born I set you apart; I appointed you as a prophet to the nations"* (Jeremiah 1:5 NIV). God knew Jeremiah before he was born, set him apart, and appointed him as a prophet to the nations. As God knew Jeremiah, God also knows you and me. He set us apart and appointed us to serve in the assignment that He established for our lives.

God chose Jeremiah. Jeremiah could have followed in the steps of his father and served as a priest, but from the very beginning, God had chosen him for something different. The Scriptures say that God chose him to serve as a prophet to the nations. The Bible makes it clear that it was God—not his family—who chose him.

Again, this reveals to us that *God chooses whom He uses;* and when God chooses, it requires obedience and discipline. Jeremiah was obedient to his call. As Isaiah 64:8 says, *"But now, O Lord, thou art our father; we are the clay, and thou our potter; and we all are the work of thy hand."* Like Jeremiah, we must be obedient to the call that God has for our lives, because as the master potter, only He knows the plans for our lives; and *He chooses whom He uses*.

God chose David, an ordinary shepherd boy who wanted to be used by the Lord. He was *"selected from the common people to be king"* (Psalm 89:19 NLT). Not even Jesse, his own father, saw his value; but God did. God chose David to become the king of Israel. God knew his heart and the limitations that he would face, but He also knew David could rise to the challenge. He knows the same about you and me and has confidence in our ability to perform any task He gives us.

God also chose Gideon. The Midianites were so cruel that the Israelites had fled to the mountains, but God called Gideon to deliver them. He told Gideon how He wanted to use him, but Gideon's response showed his concern: *"How can I save Israel? My family is the poorest in the whole Tribe of Manasseh and I am the least thought of in the entire family"* (Judges 6:15 TLB). Despite how small Gideon felt, the Lord could still see buried inside of him the qualities needed to be one of God's mighty heroes. So He replied to Gideon: *"Mighty hero, the Lord is with you!"* (Judges 6:12 NLT). It didn't matter how Gideon felt about himself, because *God chooses whom He uses*.

Sometimes we doubt our own abilities, but God knows what we are capable of doing. We cannot doubt God, because He is *"the author and finisher of our faith"* (Hebrews 12:2). God is our creator, and He has the power to mold us according to His plan. We are His clay, relying on His great abilities and knowing that the more we yield to God, the more we will come out pleasing before Him.

God Chose . . . Tracy

When God called me into His kingdom, I received the salvation that is freely given through Christ; but in order to walk in salvation, I had to be fed the Word of God, much as a newborn is fed milk. Unfortunately for me, however, the word I received wasn't from God, but from my drill sergeant screaming in my ear, because instead of serving in the army of the Lord, I joined the United States Army!

Even when we are not in God's perfect will, God still watches over us. Even though David strayed from God and sinned with Bathsheba, he repented and again pursued God and was thus considered a man after God's own heart. God had a plan for him, as long as he continued to pursue Him. Similarly, in my own case, my repentance and my pursuit of God kept me in His fold; otherwise, someone else would be writing this book!

God will never leave us nor forsake us, regardless of our actions, because God's desire for our lives is that we would become part of His family. The Bible says, *"As many as believe on Him, to them He gave the right to be called children of God"* (John 1:12). God will even soften the hearts of those whom we have hurt so that there will be no stone left unturned when we come back in repentance. The parable of the lost son in Luke 15:11–32 beautifully illustrates this point.

This parable relates the story of two sons. One day the younger son said to his father, *"Father, give me my share of your property."* So his father divided his property between his sons. Not many days after, the younger son gathered all his things together and traveled to a far country. There are many instances in the Bible where people traveled to a far country without God's blessing. In those instances, they usually got a whipping through life's experiences and ended up back where they started. This was the case in this parable.

The son who departed wasted his property with riotous living and was eventually led back home because of his circumstances and the remembrance of his father's provision. When he arrived home, his father received him unconditionally, with a loving heart and complete forgiveness.

In the same manner that this father received his son, our Father in heaven will receive us if we travel to a far country without His blessing but want to return. God is always working behind the scenes in our lives, but we must be quick to repent and ready to pursue Him so that we live as God has chosen and purposed—before we were even formed in our mother's womb.

Similarly, even though I strayed from God's call for over twenty years, God, as the master potter, was concerned for me, just like He is for all the lost. God has a plan for everyone, but we must yield to His call in order to be used by Him. It wasn't until twenty years after my initial acceptance of Jesus as my Lord and Savior, while I was serving as an insurance agent, that I began to realize the plan that God had for my life. After asking God, seeking His face, and knocking at His door every morning, I realized that I wasn't living in God's perfect will. But once I began to pursue God as David pursued Him, I began to see the steps that God had ordered for my life.

The Bible says, *"The steps of a good man are ordered by the Lord, and He delights in his way"* (Psalm 37:23 NKJV). To walk in the steps that God has ordered, we must be in right standing with Him and continuously pursue His will for our lives. We come into right standing with God when we first seek Him and His righteousness; then we can begin walking in His perfect will as opposed to His permissive will.

As I continued in prayer, I began to seek the area of work that I believed God was directing me toward, but I didn't get it right the first time. In fact, I don't know many people who do get it right the first time, because God is continuously molding us and burning off the areas of our lives that are unlike Him.

One area I began to look into was the field of counseling. I pursued this area because I thought God was leading me to it so that I could help people in the church and community. I thought that this area of work would lead to my being in God's perfect will for my life. To work in this area, I was required to enroll in a counseling program. After attending a six-week assessment course, I was accepted into the program. Although I was happy about being accepted, I had no peace in my heart to continue.

After a week of prayer and fasting, on the first day of class, I realized that this line of work was not what God had called me to do at this point in time. I came to this conclusion because I had no peace in the decision. The Bible, however, says, *"You will keep in perfect peace him whose mind is steadfast, because he trusts in you. Trust in the LORD forever, for the LORD, the LORD, is the Rock eternal"* (Isaiah 26:3–4 NIV). Because of the absence of peace in my heart, the next day I submitted a letter of withdrawal from the program. From this experience, I learned that when there is no peace in a decision, it's probably not God's perfect will for your life.

After this revelation, I did not give up but continued to pray and fast in search of God's perfect will. God has a plan and a purpose for everything that we do in life, and when certain events occur they are often clues to His will. So I reviewed my previous jobs and assignments and realized that I had completed twenty years of service in the military and then nine years as an insurance and financial-services agent. Looking back, I saw that God had used the military to establish discipline in my life and to teach me how to work with different cultures, religions, and people. He used the insurance and financial-services business to help me learn how to witness to people and build organizations from the ground up. All along, God had been developing my skills and eventually led me to His perfect will for my life, which, I believe, is to minister to people as an ambassador to the nations.

As God called Abraham, Samuel, Gideon, David, and Jeremiah, God also called me to serve as an ambassador to the nations. In other words, I am "Christ's International Ambassador" (CIA), as Dr. Patricia Bailey of Master's Touch Ministries states in her book *Our Unclaimed Inheritance: The Hidden World of African-Americans in Missions*.[8] I did not understand why God would want to use me in this capacity, since I had no experience in the area of missions, but 1 Corinthians 1:27–29 shed some light on it. Verse 27 in this passage says, *"But God has chosen the foolish things of the world to put to shame the wise, and God has chosen the weak things of the world to put to shame the things which are mighty"* (NKJV). In other words, *God chooses whom He uses*—not man, but God.

Jeremiah 18:1–6 speaks of God's sovereign choice:

The word which came to Jeremiah from the Lord, saying, Arise, and go down to the potter's house, and there I will cause thee to hear my words. Then I went down to the potter's house, and, behold, he wrought a work on the wheels. And the vessel that he made of clay was marred in the hand of the potter: so he made it again another vessel, as seemed good to the potter to make it. Then the word of the Lord came to me, saying, O house of Israel, cannot I do with you as

*this potter? saith the LORD. Behold, as the
clay is in the potter's hand, so are ye in mine
hand, O house of Israel.*

We are all in God's hands, and it is God who
chooses how someone will be molded or broken. He
is the potter; the clay, which is our bodies, is in His
hands. In the case of Jeremiah, God chose him to
serve as a prophet to the nations.

Once I realized that my call was to go into
other countries to serve as a witness for Christ, I
learned that this position was that of a missionary, or
someone sent by God. In my experience, however,
missionaries were nicely dressed ladies of the church
who wore all-white uniforms and white hats. These
ladies usually sat in their own section of the church,
and from what I observed, they worked in the church
doing good for people. Since I had never seen men
dressed in white and serving in this capacity, I began
to wonder if I had really heard from God!

Nevertheless, obeying God's call is very important, so I began searching for more information about
missionaries. As I began my research, I discovered
that the missionary ladies of the church were not the
same missionaries that God had called me to be a part
of. I also discovered, much to my surprise, that the
word *missions* or *missionary* is not found anywhere
in the Bible.

Even though these are good words, it is important to have a clear understanding of what these
words actually mean. The word *missions* comes from
the Latin word *mitto*, which means, "I send." God's

ultimate purpose is to make Himself known, and to achieve this purpose, God sends certain people on a mission. Those whom God sends are called missionaries, which means "sent ones." So missionaries are people sent by God to serve as God's messengers, witnesses, and spokesmen.

Ironically, the word that the Bible uses for "one who is sent" is the word *apostle*. Although *apostle* is the correct biblical word for someone who is sent, the word *missionary* is more commonly used by people in the church. Regardless of the term used, God does speak of sending people. John 17:18 says, *"As you sent Me into the world, I also have sent them into the world"* (NKJV). John 20:21 also speaks of sending people: *"So Jesus said to them again, 'Peace to you! As the Father has sent Me, I also send you' "* (NKJV).

God Chose . . . Linda

My wife, Linda, was first called to serve in God's kingdom when she was eleven years old, and she received the infilling of the Holy Spirit when she was thirteen. At a very young age, Linda remembers having dreams of feeding the hungry and caring for the poor, not knowing that one day she would be living out her dream as a missionary. At the age of fifteen, while attending Emmanuel Christian Center in San Francisco, California, Linda realized that missions would someday become an integral part of her life.

The church Linda attended was led by a global-minded pastor who supported and invited missionaries from around the world to speak and teach on their experiences on the mission field. Being part of a church with a foundation for supporting missions and hearing the stories told by visiting missionaries caused Linda to begin to see herself serving on the mission field one day. Even while she was a teenager, God was developing her ability to serve and lead. Linda attended youth camp, later served as a youth leader, instructed a young ladies' Bible group, participated in several choirs, and later in life served as a Sunday school teacher. These were just some of the activities that she was involved in that laid the foundation for what God was preparing for her to do later on the mission field.

In 1983, Linda went on her first mission trip, which was to Haiti. The vision that God had placed in her heart during childhood finally materialized as she fed hungry people and witnessed to lost souls. This was just the beginning of her continuous service in missions. Even though her next mission trip didn't occur until eleven years later, Linda continued to grow in the Lord. God was slowly molding her to serve on the mission field. During this time, she attended a missions training course at World Outreach Church for All Nations in Tucker, Georgia. This course was instrumental in teaching her the fundamental principles that she draws on, even to this day, while serving on the mission field.

In 1997, before I ever knew her, Linda and her family moved to Africa and lived in Harare,

Zimbabwe, for over eighteen months before returning to the United States. The experiences she gained while serving on the mission field and her desire to reach lost souls and feed the hungry remain with her to this day. That is why she continues to go on short-term mission trips every year.

Linda continues to serve God with all her heart and soul and is the cofounder of Heart of Compassion Missionary Ministries. The vision of this ministry is to provide for and teach orphans, empower the poor, feed the hungry, and train and inspire other believers to serve in missions.

Called to Witness

God uses our experiences in life to train and develop us for His purpose. He used my experiences in the military to prepare me to lead and work on the foreign mission field, and He developed Linda early in life to provide her with a solid foundation to serve as an example for inspiring others to take part in missions. Together we serve as witnesses for Christ.

Regardless of what someone has done in life and regardless of title or current position, *God chooses whom He uses*. Of course, not every believer is called to go and live permanently in another country or even to go on a short-term mission, but we are all called to serve as witnesses for Christ. We each have an assignment with a vision to fill.

Many times we look at the position that we serve in as being below our level of expertise rather than looking at how God is molding us. One minister said it this way, "If you think you are too big to do something small for God then you are probably too small to do something big for Him. If God can trust you with something small, He can trust you with something big." This also reminds me of what the Bible says in Matthew 25:21, it reads: *"His lord said to him, 'Well done, good and faithful servant; you were faithful over a few things, I will make you ruler over many things. Enter into the joy of your lord.' "* (NKJV). We must be faithful servants and good stewards over all the provisions that God has given to us so that we can accomplish His mandate.

Some people serve by giving provision for the vision, while others go to fulfill the vision; but both are equally important. John 13:16 says, *"Most assuredly, I say to you, a servant is not greater than his master; nor is he who is sent greater than he who sent him."* We are all important because we are all called to witness for Christ. Whether we are the one who sends or the person designated to go, God has a plan and a purpose for each of us. But we will not realize our assignment or calling unless we pray and read God's Word to hear what He has for our lives. As the potter molds the clay, God also molds us in whatever fashion He chooses, because *God chooses whom He uses*—and He has chosen us to serve as His Christian International Ambassadors to the nations.

Chapter 5

A Vision for the World

Where there is no vision, the people perish:
but he that keepeth the law, happy is he.
                                    —Proverbs 29:18

The Church is making advances in getting the gospel to other countries. This is exactly what Jesus said would happen: ***"And this gospel of the kingdom shall be preached in all the world for a witness unto all nations; and then shall the end come"*** (Matthew 24:14). As we look at this verse, we can conclude that the missionary task will be completed when Christians have witnessed "unto all nations." In other words, before Christ returns, Christians will have preached the gospel everywhere, and all people groups will have had the opportunity to accept or reject Christ as their Lord and Savior.

But in order for the task to be completed, we must have a global vision, more so now than at any other time in the history of the Church. This day and hour are ever so important because there are so many people living in darkness without having had an opportunity to hear the gospel. As I listen to preachers in the church, however, I hear far too many messages centered on programs to keep believers inside the church rather than thrusting them outside the church as part of a global outreach plan. The problem is that many church leaders do not have an effective global vision to reach the unreached peoples of the world. Sadly, they are satisfied with having a well-planned community outreach program while almost two billion people remain outside the reach of the gospel.

We Need a Vision

It seems as though many of us have forgotten the vision that God gave Paul: *"And a vision appeared to Paul in the night. A man of Macedonia stood and pleaded with him, saying, 'Come over to Macedonia and help us' "* (Acts 16:9 NKJV). We need to see what Paul saw that night. When God brought a man to stand before Paul, he heard the man say, "Come and help us." Every Christian needs to hear and see that vision. We must hear lost souls crying out, "Come and help us."

When Paul saw the vision, he followed it. The results were profound. People were saved, entire families were baptized, an earthquake shook open a prison cell, and many prayers were answered. And in the midst of all these miracles, the work of God continued to be preached throughout the region. If we want to see the same results, we must ask God to give us a vision of lost souls like the one He gave Paul.

We must ask God for a global vision that will have a great impact on the world. Apostle Paul, the most prominent missionary in the New Testament, gave his life in obedience to Jesus' mandate. He understood that nothing else mattered, and his entire life was wrapped up in it. He said, *"My ambition has always been to preach the Good News where the name of Christ has never been heard, rather than where a church has already been started by someone else. I have been following the plan spoken of in the Scriptures, where it says, 'Those who have never been told about him will see, and those who have never heard of him will understand' "* (Romans 15:20–21 NLT). As we study the Bible, this same vision will become so real to us that we will have a burning desire to bring people out of darkness and into the light of Christ.

We need a vision like Paul Cuffee's, one of the first African-Americans to lead a missions effort to evangelize Africa. In the early nineteenth century, Paul Cuffee advocated populating the western coast of Africa with free black missionaries from America who would live there and proclaim the gospel.

We need a vision like William Carey's, a cobbler, preacher, and missionary with a vision to reach Hindus throughout India. After leaving his home in England, William Carey gave forty-one years of service to India. He published the first complete translation of the Bible in the Bengali language.

We need a vision like David Livingstone's, a Scotsman and a pathfinder in Africa. Livingstone had a vision to find a path to the heart of Africa in order to reach lost souls.

We need a vision like Lott Carey's, the first African-American missionary on record to go to Africa. Instrumental in organizing the Richmond African Missionary Society, Lott Carey was interested in missionary work among the African natives. Through his efforts, the first church in Liberia, Providence Baptist Church, was established, and it ministered to native tribes.

Church leaders must now look to the bold visions of Apostle Paul, Paul Cuffee, William Carey, David Livingstone, Lott Carey, and many other missionaries of long ago as inspiration to encourage and support global outreach to the nations. Proverbs 29:18 says, *"Where there is no vision, the people perish: but he that keepeth the law, happy is he."* We need a vision that focuses on reaching lost souls living in refugee camps, in nations of severe poverty, in areas subjected to political genocide, and in war-torn countries where religious wars have decimated the will of the people. Church leaders and mission organizations alike must unite to develop a global outreach strategy to reach unreached souls by establishing church-planting movements that will transform entire nations.

Take Action

In Acts 2:17, the Bible says, *"And it shall come to pass in the last days, saith God, I will pour out of my Spirit upon all flesh: and your sons and your daughters shall prophesy, and your young men shall see visions, and your old men shall dream dreams."* It's time for church leaders to take action and bring to reality the visions and dreams of believers in the twenty-first century. Church leaders must recognize the sense of urgency to reach lost souls by establishing a globally coordinated training and support effort in areas of the world where outreach is still greatly needed.

Leader training and education is necessary to give leaders a better understanding of what it will take to develop a global vision, and this begins with having an understanding of the word *vision*. The definition of *vision* from the *Merriam-Webster's Dictionary* includes several aspects: (1) "a manifestation to the senses of something immaterial"; (2) "unusual discernment or foresight"; and (3) "the act or power of seeing."[9] From a biblical point of view, vision is a reflection of what God wants to accomplish through a believer. God will use believers who have a vision to reach the nations and to go into uncharted areas of the world.

A global vision entails seeing the world through the eyes of Christ. We need to see God's worldwide purpose as it was first revealed in His promise to Abraham. A global vision also requires maintaining focus through encouragement, unity, and education.

Global vision requires the obedience of strong church leaders working jointly together with all believers in pursuit of accomplishing God's purpose for people. In the Old Testament, God said to Moses, ***"But command Joshua, and encourage him and strengthen him; for he shall go over before this people, and he shall cause them to inherit the land which you will see"*** (Deuteronomy 3:28 NKJV). God's emphasis on obedient and strong leadership was apparent through this decision to allow Joshua rather than Moses to lead the people into the Promised Land. Even though Moses had been the one to lead the children of Israel out of Egypt, God still exacted a price on his earlier disobedience.

Similarly, God requires that we remain obedient to His Word and obey the commandments that He has set before us. Even when our circumstances change, we must trust God. We must have the same trust and faith in God as Joshua and Caleb had when they brought back their report of the Promised Land (Numbers 13:25-33). Like them, we must believe the vision that God gives us and have faith that it will manifest in due season. As we do this, we will begin to see the world through the eyes of Christ, and God's purpose for our lives will be fulfilled, just as He planned it before we were ever formed in our mothers' wombs.

Developing an intimate relationship with God will lead to a better understanding of God's global vision. Then, as church leaders begin to share God's global vision with other believers and come together in prayer, God will give provision for the vision to accomplish His mission of reaching lost souls.

Church leaders must spearhead the thrust for global outreach by getting people to participate in the support of missionaries who have already answered the call to go to the mission field. In the New Testament, Paul instructs us, *"Therefore I remind you to stir up the gift of God which is in you through the laying on of my hands"* (2 Timothy 1:6 NKJV). God wants all believers to rekindle the embers and fan the flame of passion for lost souls by supporting the global vision.

In the book of Jeremiah, the Scriptures say, *"For I know the thoughts that I think toward you, says the Lord, thoughts of peace and not of evil, to give you a future and a hope"* (Jeremiah 29:11 NKJV). God has a positive, expected end for our lives. When God calls us, He also gives us a vision—a vision that we must reach for, hold on to, and run with. Without a vision from God, we can easily find ourselves going down a road that God did not ordain, thus leading to a life of toil and dissatisfaction. This is why we must seek God to know the vision He has purposed for us for while living on this earth.

God Gives Vision

How do we get vision? God gives vision and will reveal Himself to us when we read the Word of God, pray, and fast. If we are not in His Word, we will always be second-guessing ourselves to see whether God has actually spoken to us. In Matthew 6:33, the

Bible says, *"But seek ye first the kingdom of God, and his righteousness; and all these things shall be added unto you."* When we seek God first, our spirit will be open to receive the vision that God preordained before we were even born. When we seek God first, we will realize the purpose that God has for our life. When we seek God first, we will be able to hear the Voice of God.

God can speak to us in a number of different ways. First and foremost, He speaks through His written word. This is His primary voice, and despite this, so many of us choose not to hear from Him. We make this choice when we don't bother to open the Bible. We must, therefore, spend time in reading and seeking to understand what God is saying through His Word.

The writer to the Hebrews reminds us that God also speaks to us through His Son: *"Long ago God spoke many times and in many ways to our ancestors through the prophets. And now in these final days, he has spoken to us through his Son. God promised everything to the Son as an inheritance, and through the Son he created the universe"* (Hebrews 1:1-2 NLT).

Other ways that God speaks to us is through dreams, visions, and angels. In Luke 1:19 the Bible says, *"And the angel answering said unto him, I am Gabriel, that stand in the presence of God; and am sent to speak unto thee, and to show thee these glad tidings."*

God also speaks through the Holy Spirit. As Comforter and Counselor, the Holy Spirit leads, guides, and directs us with the vision God has placed in our hearts. The Bible says, ***"However, when He, the Spirit of truth, has come, He will guide you into all truth; for He will not speak on His own authority, but whatever He hears He will speak; and He will tell you things to come"*** (John 16:13 NKJV). God has made His dwelling within us and speaks to our hearts through the inner Voice of God. As we seek God first and position ourselves to hear the Voice of God, God's vision will be revealed to us.

Our Vision

The vision of Heart of Compassion Missionary Ministries is to establish a global ministry that will do its part in fulfilling the Great Commission by empowering people in unreached areas of the world as well as teaching and training people from all nations to spread the gospel of Jesus Christ through foreign missions. The world is full of great need, and there is much work to be done. People are still living in refugee camps in some areas of the world. People have been targeted for genocide because of differing religions in other areas. People are dying from starvation, and people are dying from HIV/AIDS at extraordinary rates because of the lack of available medication.

A great number of the people with the greatest needs live in the poorest of the poor countries of the world and have never had an opportunity to hear the gospel. But as we establish our goals and objectives to accomplish the vision that God has placed in our

hearts, people will be saved, delivered, and empow-
ered through Christ as we commit to reaching people
and touching lives around the world.

The Challenges

Many people are not living the quality of life
that God intended for them. For example, God has
given people wisdom to create medicine to help the
sick, creativity to think up witty inventions to grow
wealth, the ability to write books to give knowledge
and understanding, and the insight to develop trans-
portation and construct houses and buildings to live
and work in so that they can have a better quality of
life. By reaching the unreached people of the world,
we will thus offer them the opportunity to not only
live a Christ-filled life but to also benefit from the
wisdom that God gives so liberally to anyone who
asks.

In the book of Psalms, the Bible says, *"He shall
call upon Me, and I will answer him; I will be with
him in trouble; I will deliver him and honor him.
With long life I will satisfy him, and show him My
salvation"* (Psalm 91:15–16 NKJV). When we call
on God, He will add long life, but so many people
have died because they had no opportunity to hear
the call for salvation. However, for those privileged
to hear the call, God's path is a path of favor: *"For
whoever finds me finds life, and obtains favor from
the LORD"* (Proverbs 8:35 NKJV).

When we trust and hope in God to reach the peoples
of the world, He will send people with knowledge

and understanding to help improve literacy rates in illiterate lands. He will send people to disease-prone regions to give instruction concerning basic hygiene to decrease the infant mortality rate. He will send people to help stop the spread of malaria by implementing mosquito abatement efforts. By reaching the unreached population of the world, we will give them an opportunity to live longer, more meaningful lives through Christ.

Although efforts are being made to reach those who do not know Christ, much more work still needs to be done. We cannot yet say that everyone has had an opportunity to experience the same favor and quality of life that believers in Christ experience. According to the World Health Organization's Mortality Country Fact Sheet 2006, the life expectancy of men in Afghanistan is 42 years; in Guinea, 52; Ethiopia, 49; Mozambique, 44; Congo, 53; Nigeria, 45; and Zimbabwe, 37.[10] These countries are just a few of the many countries where people have a short life expectancy, and they also represent some of the countries with the greatest need for global evangelism.

The short life expectancy can be attributed to many causes, but one likely reason is that people in undeveloped countries do not have access to adequate health care. Additionally, people who do not have a relationship with Christ are not living the lives that God intended for them, and because of a lack of knowledge, they end up going in a direction that costs them their lives.

Hosea 4:6 says, *"My people are destroyed for lack of knowledge."* According to the International

Bulletin of Missionary Research, dated January 2008, research conducted by David B. Barrett and Todd M. Johnson revealed that there are approximately 1,094,278,000 adults in the world who are illiterate.[11] These people can't read the Bible, a tract, or even the instructions on a box of oatmeal. In this modern-day society, this shouldn't be the case. What is even sadder is that between 2000 and mid-2008, the number of illiterate grew by over 100 million. This is just one reason why it is so important for the Church to come together in developing a united strategy for global evangelism. We must go outside our local communities to reach the lost and help those who are illiterate and need assistance.

What is even more alarming is the fact, according to a report by the United Nations Children's Fund (UNICEF), that 9.7 million children every year die before their fifth birthday.[12] Most of these children live in developing countries and die from a disease or a combination of diseases that are easily prevented or treated. For example, if more children simply had access to antibiotics for pneumonia or a simple mix of salts and sugars for diarrhea, many lives could be saved.

Also, in children of this age, malnutrition is another contributing factor for half of these deaths. When you think of all the food discarded by grocery stores in developed countries, you are hard-pressed to come up with a reason why an entire generation of children should die because there isn't enough food on their tables! Thus it is important that the body of Christ have a global vision and extend the hand of

Christ, which represents His provision, to those countries in desperate need of food and other essentials.

Health care professionals, especially those who know Christ, are also in great demand in undeveloped countries. These professionals can play a major role in global evangelism and serve as witnesses for Christ by saving lives both physically and spiritually. Statistics from the 2004 World Health Organization revealed that in the United States, there were over 730,801 doctors, 463,663 dentists, and 2.6 million nurses. In India, with three and a half times the number of people, there were fewer doctors, nurses, and dentists in proportion to the population. In Mozambique, with about 20 million people, there were approximately 514 doctors, 159 dentists, and 6,183 nurses. In Guinea, with almost 7 million people, there were 987 doctors, 60 dentists, and 4,408 nurses.[13] Opportunities abound for health care professionals from the United States and other developed countries to serve on short-term mission trips, but the appeal must be made through prayer and fasting to place the desire on the hearts of these professionals.

Overcoming the Challenges

How do we overcome these challenges? First, we must support and send more missionaries to the areas where the unreached people groups are located. In doing so, we must be careful in our approach. We cannot go to a country and expect to impose a colonial-minded plan to change people in accordance with our societal norms. We must reach the unreached with the love of Christ as our foundation.

Additionally, Christians must have a united vision for the twenty-first century, with new goals and objectives. We must recruit, train, and educate indigenous people to become doctors, dentists, and nurses in undeveloped countries while also sending people from developed countries on short-term and long-term mission trips. We must pray that the Lord will reveal His will in the area of global outreach to church leaders and other members of the body of Christ. We must also pray that all believers will see the church as a training ground for missionaries and that provision for the vision will be made available to send and support those who have been called to serve in missions.

We must also unite as the body of Christ and use all available resources to direct the distribution of food to needy countries and to help those countries that can no longer afford to buy food because of soaring food prices. Although there may be an abundance of food in some countries, people are starving in many other countries.

Finally, we must have the same passion that Jesus had for lost souls. Matthew 9:36 records, *"But when he saw the multitudes, he was moved with compassion on them, because they fainted, and were scattered abroad, as sheep having no shepherd."* When Jesus saw the multitudes, He did not see them as statistics—He saw them as lost souls. We must look beyond our needs and use the resources of the church to help impoverished people and empower them through the Word of God. The opportunity to reach people around the world exists now more than ever before, but a strategic, global vision is necessary, because *"where there is no vision, the people perish"* (Proverbs 29:18).

Chapter 6

Pray for More Laborers

Then He said to His disciples, "The harvest truly is plentiful, but the laborers are few. Therefore pray the Lord of the harvest to send out laborers into His harvest."
— Matthew 9:37–38 NKJV

Fulfillment in Christ

There are many people on earth who are seeking the true meaning of life but are not finding fulfillment in what the world has to offer. That's because true fulfillment can come only through Christ. People may find temporary fulfillment in their professions or in a hobby, but God is the only one who can provide everlasting love, joy, and peace. People can seek and search throughout the world, but they will never find what they are looking for in their professions, possessions, or hobbies.

This unrelenting search for fulfillment reminds me of a song I heard while on the mission field in Zimbabwe. The song speaks of people looking, seeking, and searching for someone or something in the world that can provide satisfaction. It concludes with the truth that satisfaction cannot be found in the world, but only through a relationship with Christ. The song also represents the essence of our eternal instinct to continue searching within ourselves until we uncover the purpose that God has for our lives. This purpose, however, can be discovered only as we seek God through His Word, search within ourselves through fasting, and communicate with Him through prayer.

More than two billion souls are still looking, seeking, and searching to find purpose in life, so we must pray for more laborers. Even though many Christians have answered the call to personal salvation, we must pray that they will also be sensitive to answer God's call to serve on the mission field. More than any other time in the history of mankind, we are now in the season to gather the souls that are ready for harvest. Although it may sound like an easy task, we do have an enemy with a mission to steal, kill, and destroy the harvest before it can be reaped; this is why we must pray fervently for more laborers.

Prayer Is the Active Ingredient

Every day, people who do not know Christ are dying without the opportunity to receive eternal life. There are not enough laborers on the mission field;

the harvest is ready for picking, but the laborers are few. This situation is no different from leaving ripened fruit on a tree to rot because there are not enough laborers to pick it. God has already prepared the harvest through our prayers, but it can quickly rot if we are not praying for more laborers to go and reap the harvest.

James 5:16 proclaims, *"The effectual fervent prayer of a righteous man availeth much."* We must continue to pray fervently for more laborers, because God has already prepared the food and set the table. But He is waiting for us to invite people to come to the table and eat.

E. M. Bounds, a man of prayer, wrote the following in his book entitled *Essentials of Prayer:*

Our Lord's plan for securing workers in the foreign missionary field is the same plan He set on foot for obtaining preachers. It is by the process of praying. It is the prayer plan as distinguished from all man-made plans. These mission workers are to be "sent men." God must send them. They are God-called, divinely moved to this great work. They are inwardly moved to enter the harvest fields of the world and gather sheaves for the heavenly garners. Men do not choose to be missionaries any more than they choose to be preachers. God sends out labourers in His harvest field in answer to the prayers of His church. Here is the Divine plan as set forth by our Lord:

"But when he saw the multitudes, he was moved with compassion on them, because they fainted, and were as sheep having no shepherd. Then saith he unto his disciples, The harvest truly is plenteous, but the labourers are few. Pray ye, therefore, the Lord of the harvest that he will send forth labourers into his harvest" (Matthew 9:36–38).

It is the business of the home church to do the praying. It is the Lord's business to call and send forth the labourers. The Lord does not do the praying. The Church does not do the calling. And just as our Lord's compassions were aroused by the sight of multitudes, weary, hungry, and scattered, exposed to evils, as sheep having no shepherd, so whenever the Church has eyes to see the vast multitudes of earth's inhabitants, descendants of Adam, weary in soul, living in darkness, and wretched and sinful, will it be moved to compassion, and begin to pray the Lord of the harvest to send forth labourers into His harvest.[14]

It is evident from reading this passage that the Church, prayer, and missions must be joined together in the same way that God joins a husband and wife in marriage. As the Church prays for unreached peoples of the world, God will act on those prayers and tie His mission to the Church. To accomplish His mission, the Church must now pray for more laborers to be sent. Prayer is essential for God to act.

Matthew 7:7–8 says, *"Ask, and it will be given to you; seek, and you will find; knock, and it will be opened to you. For everyone who asks receives, and he who seeks finds, and to him who knocks it will be opened."* God will send missionaries, but we must ask. The essential ingredient for accomplishing His mission is asking in our prayers; it is the active ingredient for God.

Prayer is asking God. Prayer is letting Him know that our hearts are in line with His heart. Then, as Jesus assured His followers, if we are persistent and sincere, He is able to provide the means for the otherwise impossible. Far too often, however, Christians do not have because they do not ask, or they ask with selfish motives (James 4:2–3). Like a human father, the heavenly Father seeks to teach His children patience, persistence, and diligence. He wants to know that they really have the same desire that He has for people who don't know Him; that's why we must continue to ask for more laborers.

Prayer serves as the magnet that will draw more laborers into His harvest field. In Matthew 9:37–38, when Jesus speaks of the laborers being few, a question arises: why are there so few laborers? I don't know the answer, but it's interesting to note that rather than recruiting more laborers, Jesus commands His disciples to *"pray that the Lord of the harvest will send forth laborers into His fields."* As the Church *really* gets serious about conducting global missions, we will hear of more churches praying for the Lord of the harvest to send out more laborers. It is the Lord of the harvest who will select and prepare the laborers, but as E. M. Bounds stated, we must make our request known through prayer.

The Harvest Is Ripe

Approximately one-third of the world is totally ignorant of Christianity, Christ, and the gospel. This represents approximately two billion people, even after two thousand years under the mandate to go and make disciples of all nations. Although progress is being made, there are not large numbers of Christian missionaries targeting the unreached groups or enough income being spent by churches to reach them. We must pray that the laborers are sensitive to hearing the call of God so that they will go to locations where an impact can be made.

It is important that we become familiar with the strongholds binding billions of people throughout the world. Some people, for instance, worship spirits in everything they see, such as the stars, the moon, the sun, and the sky. Others practice witchcraft and believe in the power of many fetishes. Additionally, people of other religions worship animals, such as snakes, rats, monkeys, tigers, or anything else that fits with their religious beliefs.

There are billions of people in this world, but we are all God's creation: the saved, those who have already accepted Jesus as their Lord and Savior; and the unsaved, the lost billions who have yet to hear the gospel. Those who are lost and outside God's kingdom languish in the harvest fields of the world, so we must pray for more laborers to go out into the field to reach them.

The Bible clearly states, *"The Lord is not slack concerning His promise, as some count slackness, but is longsuffering toward us, not willing that any should perish but that all should come to repentance"* (2 Peter 3:9 NKJV). Everyone should have an opportunity to come to repentance, and if the Great Commission is to be fulfilled, we must pray that God sends out more missionaries. A prayer that believers can pray in order to fulfill the command to go into the world and preach the gospel is the Lord's Prayer, found in Matthew 6:9–13. When we pray, *"Thy kingdom come,"* as stated in verse 10, we are in effect praying for God to send out more laborers to serve in His kingdom; and to fulfill this request, God will have to send more laborers to the mission field. Every day as part of our prayer time, we must pray the Lord of the harvest to send out more laborers into His harvest. And as we pray the Lord's Prayer, God will acknowledge our prayers and will indeed send more laborers to the mission fields of the world.

We must continue to pray and not grow weary in praying for more laborers. The Bible says, *"The fruit of the righteous is a tree of life; and he that winneth souls is wise"* (Proverbs 11:30). We are all here because Jesus, the Good Shepherd, has already gathered us into His flock. He saw us when we were helpless. He told one of His followers to pray for our salvation. And because someone prayed, He sent forth laborers to declare the good news to us. The

Word of God declares, *"You are My friends if you do whatever I command you"* (John 15:14 NKJV). As Christians, we must be wise and do as God commanded—win souls for Christ!

The responsibility to spread the gospel belongs to every believer. In Ezekiel 3:17–18, we read, *"Son of man, I have made you a watchman for the house of Israel; therefore hear a word from My mouth, and give them warning from Me: When I say to the wicked, 'You shall surely die,' and you give him no warning, nor speak to warn the wicked from his wicked way, to save his life, that same wicked man shall die in his iniquity; but his blood I will require at your hand"* (NKJV). We cannot neglect our responsibility of serving as witnesses for Christ, because we will be held accountable for the blood of the lost.

The task of spreading the gospel rests in the hands of all believers. We cannot do as we choose; we must do as God has commanded. We must continue to pray for more laborers to proclaim the gospel, and we must also pray for those who are already on the mission field. Apostle Paul gives some specific prayer requests that we can pray for all missionaries: *"Pray that I will proclaim this message as clearly as I should [and that I] live wisely among those who are not believers, and make the most of every opportunity"* (Colossians 4:2–4 NLT). We must pray that missionaries will have opportunities to share the gospel and proclaim it clearly and that they will live wisely among all people.

Participation in global missions is the responsibility of every believer. Praying the Lord of the harvest to send out workers is the foundation to fulfilling God's plan for all the people on the earth. In response to our prayers, the Lord will bring people to repentance and faith and place them into His Church. Then will His *name*, His *kingdom*, and His *will* become central.

Our desire for God, His kingdom, and His will, along with our gratefulness for receiving His mercy, is what will inspire us to pray. E. M. Bounds, in his book *Essentials of Prayer*, said this:

Missionaries, like ministers, are born of praying people. A praying church begets labourers in the harvest-field of the world. The scarcity of missionaries argues a non-praying church. It is all right to send trained men to the foreign field, but first of all they must be God-sent. The sending is the fruit of prayer. As praying men are the occasion of sending them, so in turn the workers must be praying men. And the prime mission of these praying missionaries is to convert prayerless heathen men into praying men. Prayer is the proof of their calling, their Divine credentials, and their work.[15]

We must continue to pray for a praying church and for more intercessors. Intercession is the place where we pray to God for the sake of another person or for a corporate cause, and it is critical for the body of Christ to move forward. Even in the days of Isaiah, this need for intercession was noted*: "And he saw that there was no man, and wondered that there was no intercessor"* (Isaiah 59:16).

We desperately need more intercessors in the church, so we must pray. Only with more intercessors can we have a thriving church movement. Then, as we pray, the Lord of the harvest will send forth laborers because it is His harvest. We must pray that God will touch the hearts of those who are called to go. We must also pray that there will be people who will give provision for the vision to support missionaries as spiritual needs are met in His harvest field.

Chapter 7

Moved with Compassion

*When he saw the crowds, he had compassion
on them, because they were harassed and
helpless, like sheep without a shepherd.*

—Matthew 9:36 NIV

Heart of Compassion Missionaries Ministries
was established through the inspiration of God
and from the desire that Linda and I have for the
lost to come to repentance, thereby glorifying God.
It is our vision to demonstrate the compassion that
God has for lost souls by the giving of our time and
finances. As we prepare to go on yet another mission
trip, we are reminded in the Bible of the compassion that Jesus had in feeding the hungry, healing the
sick, casting out demons, and ministering to the lost.
We must follow the footsteps of Jesus, imitating His
example as He fed the four thousand and later the
five thousand hungry people. God's compassion for

people is obvious, and we must follow the example that was established for all people through the Son of God, Jesus.

Jesus was moved with compassion. The word *compassion* in *Merriam-Webster's Dictionary* is defined as *"a desire to free others from their suffering."* It also means "a sympathetic consciousness of others' distress with a desire to alleviate it."[16] God's desire is to free all people from suffering.

His compassion, however, could best be described as empathy, not sympathy. The word *empathy* is used to describe someone who has actually experienced the same or a similar situation to someone else and can thus fully relate. God is full of empathy for our situations in life because He experienced life on earth through His Son, Jesus, who lived among us in human form. As a result, God identifies and understands our circumstances, feelings, emotions, and motives.

God's compassion comes to life in His character. He has compassion for people who have faith in Him, who believe and trust in Him, who are willing to repent to Him, who are in need, who are kind, who perform good deeds, or who have yet to realize that He is God. His compassion is limitless and all-encompassing.

During a recent mission trip to Zimbabwe in October 2008, Linda and I were moved with compassion for the hundreds of thousands of people who live in impoverished conditions. Zimbabwe is currently experiencing a dire economic crisis, with unemployment over 80 percent, most manufacturing at a standstill, and basic foods in short supply. Zimbabwe was once one of the richest countries in Africa but now has descended into economic chaos.

When Linda and I hear that Zimbabwe has the highest inflation rate in the world, we are moved with compassion. When we hear that HIV/AIDS has devastated families and entire generations, leaving thousands of children homeless because of the death of a parent, we are moved with compassion. And this compassion dictates that we take action through prayer, fasting, and giving our time to help the people of that country to empower themselves through applying kingdom principles.

Linda and I were also moved with compassion as we ministered to people at the Fothergill Island fishing camp, located in a remote area called Gache Gache on Lake Kariba in Zimbabwe. From where we initially set up our base camp, it took an hour by boat to get to the island. Once we arrived on the island, we were welcomed by over three hundred men, women, and children. It was apparent from what we saw that the majority of people living on this remote island did not have basic clothing, medical supplies, or food. We decided to make a return trip the next day to try to meet some of these needs.

When we returned, we distributed shirts, pants, dresses, blouses, and shoes for men, women, and children, and we handed out canned milk and other food items to help them physically. But we also provided for them spiritually, feeding them through the Word of God. After preaching the Word on the second day, twenty men answered the call to salvation and received Christ as their Lord and Savior!

As God sends us to minister to the lost and poor around the world, we are moved with compassion, just like Jesus. Matthew 15:32 says, *"Then Jesus called his disciples unto him, and said, I have compassion on the multitude, because they continue with me now three days, and have nothing to eat: and I will not send them away fasting, lest they faint in the way."* Jesus was moved with compassion and changed the circumstances for the hungry multitude before Him. He has the same compassion for hungry people today living in Africa, in India, or anywhere else in the world.

When we follow God, He can instantly change our circumstances. Continuing in Matthew 15, Scripture says, *"And Jesus saith unto them, How many loaves have ye? And they said, Seven, and a few little fishes. And he commanded the multitude to sit down on the ground. And he took the seven loaves and the fishes, and gave thanks, and brake them, and gave to his disciples, and the disciples to the multitude. And they did all eat, and were filled: and they took up of the broken meat that was left seven baskets full"* (vv. 34–37).

In this passage, Jesus first organized the people by making them sit down in groups of fifty and then gave thanks to God before distributing the food. We must give thanks to our Father in heaven, in advance, for what He will do and what He has already done. Then, after Jesus gave thanks, the food multiplied. We must have this same kind of faith. Our problems may seem insurmountable, but if Jesus can feed over four thousand people with seven loaves and a few fish, He can do the same for any situation that we are facing. Jesus says in, John 14:12, *"Verily, verily, I say unto you, He that believeth on me, the works that I do shall he do also; and greater works than these shall he do; because I go unto my Father."* Keeping Jesus as our example, we must have the same compassion He had, and we must believe that through Him we can do even greater works.

God shows His compassion for those who believe. All you need to do is just believe that God has the power to perform miracles and God will have compassion on you. This is what happened with the leper who came to Jesus in Galilee: *"And there came a leper to him, beseeching him, and kneeling down to him, and saying unto him, If thou wilt, thou canst make me clean. And Jesus, moved with compassion, put forth his hand, and touched him, and saith unto him, I will; be thou clean. And as soon as he had spoken, immediately the leprosy departed from him, and he was cleansed"* (Mark 1:40–42).

Leprosy, much like AIDS today, was a terrifying disease, because there was no known cure. Can you imagine what it would be like if you were told that you had an incurable disease? How do you think you might respond? You would probably be fearful, depressed, and angry. I'm sure it must have been much the same for the leper in our story.

During this period of time, lepers were considered social and religious outcasts because of their disease. For the Israelites, leprosy rendered a person ceremonially unclean and forced him to live apart from others. But the man with leprosy approached

Christ and bowed before Him, thereby breaking the normal rules of society. He had probably watched from a distance and listened to the words of Christ. He saw the compassion of Christ toward others, and it gave him hope. Because of his faith, the leper experienced Jesus' compassion firsthand, as Jesus reached out and touched him, ignoring his physical condition.

Today there are many people who are seeking to experience the compassion of Christ but don't know how. Many people long to be delivered from guilt, sin, oppression, and depression but don't know how. But there are others, like the leper, who are living witnesses of Christ's compassionate delivering power. Apostle Shirley Ferguson, in her book *No Longer Bound—Freedom in Christ from the Snares of Satan*,[17] shares testimonies from people who have broken the chains of bondage and are no longer entrapped in Satan's snares. You might want to pick up a copy and read this powerful book.

As Christians, it's up to *us* to demonstrate Christ's compassion and love to those who have not yet experienced it. We do this by showing them our love and kindness. We must share the love of Christ, as He willingly shared it with us. Thank God that we have a friend in Jesus!

Jesus taught and demonstrated forgiveness and compassion through His own willingness to forgive. He shared its importance in a well-known parable found in Matthew 18:23–25: *"Therefore is the kingdom of heaven likened unto a certain king, who would take account of his servants. And*

when he had begun to reckon, one was brought unto him, who owed him ten thousand talents. But forasmuch as he had nothing with which to pay, his lord commanded him to be sold, and his wife, and children, and all that he had, and payment to be made."

Jesus' example of a servant who owed ten thousand talents is probably the equivalent of billions of dollars today. Regardless of the exact amount, the sum was so large that it was impossible for the average person to repay. So the lord of the servant commanded the servant and his family to be sold for a partial payment, a customary practice during biblical times.

The Bible continues the story in verses 26–27: **"The servant, therefore, fell down, and worshiped him, saying, Lord, have patience with me, and I will pay thee all. Then the lord of that servant was moved with compassion, and loosed him, and forgave him the debt."** The lord of the servant, moved by compassionate pity, forgave the servant his massive debt. This part of the parable illustrates God's unlimited forgiveness as He releases the debt of sin that we ourselves cannot pay; only through the compassion of Christ are we able to experience forgiveness of all our sins.

Finally, we must be moved with compassion as Jesus was moved with compassion. The Word must be in our hearts, like a burning fire. Without compassion for the lost, we will lose steam and forward motion, much like a steam locomotive that sits unmoving on the track because it has no steam to propel it forward. As Christians, it is important that we allow compassion to thrust us into the world, because if we don't, we too will be left standing still like a locomotive without steam. Compassion gives us the steam to go; compassion motivates us to keep looking, to keep moving, to keep studying the Word, and to go to places where people are searching for love, peace, and compassion in all the wrong things. As Jesus was moved with compassion to reach the lost, the hungry, and the sick, let us be moved by that same compassion to do the work mandated by our Father in heaven of reaching people and touching lives around the world.

Chapter 8

Provision for the Vision

A feast is made for laughter, and wine maketh merry: but money answereth all things.
— Ecclesiastes 10:19

To send missionaries to all nations takes money. To achieve this goal, Christians must unite as one body to work the kingdom system so that there can be provision for the vision. The Bible says in Luke 16:8, *"For the children of this world are in their generation wiser than the children of light."* People of the world know how to work the world system of making money. When you turn on the television or read the newspaper, you can see that the world system is continuously growing and building itself.

The world system operates from the premise of a consumer-driven society of buying and selling. For example, many people are fixated on owning the latest car, the biggest house, latest cell phone, and other gadgets. This thought process has trapped people into believing that the value of life is somehow linked to their possessions. We hear people say, "I wonder what he's worth," meaning, "I wonder how much money he has in the bank." People in the world system have the mistaken idea that a man's worth is based on the amount of money in his wallet.

The Bait of Satan

For Christians to be able to give provision for the vision, they must first understand what they're up against. The world system continues to take from and ensnare many of God's people by creating social and financial traps. Ads placed by some companies read as though Satan himself had written them. These ads are attempts of the adversary to lure people into more debt. They generally tell people things like, "Buy now and pay later. No payments for two years." Christians must be careful when they hear or see these kinds of ads because they represent the bait that Satan uses to keep people in debt.

The Bible warns us about Satan's evil devices: *"Be sober, be vigilant; because your adversary the devil walks about like a roaring lion, seeking whom he may devour. Resist him, steadfast in the faith, knowing that the same sufferings are experienced by your brotherhood in the world"* (1 Peter 5:8–9 NKJV).

Unfortunately, in the financial realm, many Christians get caught up in the world's way of doing things and end up becoming borrowers instead of lenders. Then when it's time to give offerings and pay tithes, these same Christians say that they don't have the money, which is true, because their money was already spent before they even received their paychecks. As a result of overspending, many Christians have in effect mortgaged their lives by having to work to pay off their debts instead of working to give to God. Remember, we must resist the tactics of the enemy by reading the Word, praying, fasting, and giving to the kingdom of God. This will keep the devourer from devouring our finances.

Christians must also realize how the world's banking system affects them every time they place money in their savings, checking, or money-market accounts. As we turn on the television or read the newspaper, we hear of banks providing financing for new casinos, adult video stores, and liquor stores, and then we wonder why the crime rates in our neighborhoods are increasing at alarming rates. We wonder why our children are not in school, why drug dealers have such an influence over our children, and why families are being pulled apart. But when we put our hard-earned money into the world's banking system, we are in effect financing the kingdom of darkness and signing our children's death sentence.

The children of light, Christians, must become wiser, because we are of a new generation, a generation in which the wealth must transfer from the wicked to the righteous people of God. We cannot allow the ways of the world to deceive us into believing that the world's banking system is the only system in which to invest our money. We must use banks and investment advisors that invest our money and its profits into Christian-owned banking systems that will redistribute profits back into God's kingdom. We must use the knowledge and wisdom that God has given us by repositioning ourselves for the transfer of wealth from the unrighteous to the righteous so that there will be provision for the vision to send missionaries to other countries to conduct community outreach and global evangelism.

The Wealth Transfer

For the vision to go forth, Christians must gain knowledge, understanding, and wisdom in how to build wealth in God's kingdom so that there will be a transfer of wealth. We must also adapt a lifestyle of excellence. In her book, *A Lifestyle of Excellence,*[18] Belinda Bush shares many details on how we can do this by going above and beyond the normal standard by having a spirit of excellence. Additionally, we must educate ourselves through the Word of God and through instruction from men and women whom God has ordained to teach kingdom principles of finance.

In *Seeding for the Billion Flow,*[19] Dr. Bill Winston reveals knowledge of how the world system uses our money to finance the world system of economics backed by Satan. If we want to advance the kingdom of God, we can no longer operate out of the world system. The Bible makes this clear: *"Whosoever therefore will be a friend of the world [system] is the enemy of God"* (James 4:4 NKJV).

If we intend to move the gospel forward by sending missionaries to empower nations and reach lost souls, we must be willing to put some time into learning kingdom principles of financing. The Bible explicitly says, ***"Owe no one anything except to love one another, for he who loves another has fulfilled the law"*** (Romans 13:8 NKJV). As we follow God and show our love by encouraging one another through the Word of God, wealth and prosperity will be drawn to us, like a newborn child drawn to its mother's breast!

We Christians realize that the world system exists, but we must also realize that we are not bound to it. God's system rules over the world's system. Although we are in the world, we are not of the world. It's sort of like a fish in the ocean. For example, even though a red snapper, a saltwater fish, lives in the ocean, the snapper itself is not salty. That's because it's not what the saltwater fish *lives in* that governs its life, but it's what the fish *allows* to live in him. In a similar fashion, as men and women of God, we must be careful whom we allow into our personal finances. Whether it be a tax advisor, insurance agent, financial advisor, or the bank where we do business, we have a choice of whom we use and where we do business. God has ordained certain men and women with understanding of how to become financially successful using God's principles of personal finance, and we should avail ourselves of their expertise.

In Deuteronomy 28:12–13, we learn that God desires to bless His people so that they will be lenders and not borrowers, the head and not the tail. We must understand that God's system is based on sowing and reaping, whereas the world's system is based on buying and selling. It is time for the body of Christ to learn how to work the system that God has placed on this earth for His people to prosper. But this will come only as we change our way of thinking. As I spoke of earlier, there must be a spiritual paradigm shift in the hearts and minds of all Christians so that there will be provision for the vision.

Reaching People to Empower Lives

As my wife and I traveled to different countries to preach the gospel, we noticed that when we later returned to many of these areas, the new believers in Christ were still struggling. It became apparent that after we reached people and led them to Christ, we had to begin teaching them how to empower themselves by using God's Word. Rather than relying on outside help to supply their needs, they had to learn to rely on God. Philippians 4:19 says, *"But my God shall supply all your need according to his riches in glory by Christ Jesus."* God will indeed supply the need, but it is important that this fundamental truth be taught to those led to Christ on the mission field. Otherwise, the missionary may appear to be their provider which is not the case.

Linda and I soon realized that the gospel doesn't stop after salvation. The Bible says that we must make disciples, which requires us to return and teach God's principles of living, including kingdom principles of financial freedom. For God to do His part, we must do our part by going.

With as much wealth as we have in the United States, there should be no lack for any of God's children throughout the world. Pastor Bankole Akinmola, in his book entitled *Heirs of the Kingdom,* states that "we've become experts at believing God to meet our own needs, without taking consideration for the needs of others."[20] As believers, we must learn to build wealth within the kingdom of God in order to empower the people of God to work the system that God has created for them.

Laid-Up Wealth

I continue to ask myself, *"How can there be so many hungry people in countries where there is an abundance of resources?"* For example, many countries in Africa have so many poor people, but at the same time, they possess a wealth of natural resources. If these resources could be placed in the right hands, however, there would be enough money to buy food to feed the entire continent. Just think, if a missionary were sent to one of these countries and through prayer had an opportunity to lead a person of influence to Christ, a wealth transfer could take place like we have never seen before!

But in order for this to happen, there must first be provision for the vision. Financing must be available to send missionaries to reach lost souls, to empower the poor, to educate people, and to demonstrate God's love. We must give to the vision that God has placed in the hearts of missionaries, pastors, and other believers with a heart for global evangelism. We must look outside our natural resources and begin to see the supernatural resources that only God can provide. When we begin to see God's global vision for His people, God will supply the provision for the vision.

Serving as Senders

Isaiah 6:8 says, *"Then I heard the Lord saying, 'Whom shall I send? Who will go for me?' And I answered, 'Here am I; send me.' "* It's understandable that not everyone is called to go to the mission field, but everyone can participate by giving provision for the vision. Those who are called to go need support in a number of areas so that they can focus on reaching the lost and not be encumbered by administrative issues back home. Opportunities abound for everyone in the church to get involved in supporting missionaries, but it's also vital that each person know his or her area of expertise. For example, you may volunteer to provide administrative support for a missionary, but if you're not administratively inclined, you may be more of a hindrance than a help. It is important to know your own gifts and abilities and then pray before volunteering assistance in any particular area.

People who are called to serve can offer support in a number of different areas. In *Serving As Senders*,[21] a book written by Neal Pirolo, the author identifies six areas of support in which those who are not called to go to the mission field can participate:

1. **Moral Support** — Providing encouragement to the missionary.
   Joshua 1:9 NKJV: *"Have I not commanded you? Be strong and of good courage; do not be afraid, nor be dismayed, for the LORD your God is with you wherever you go."*

2. **Logistical Support** — Assisting in administrative matters.
   2 Timothy 4:13 NKJV: *"Bring the cloak that I left with Carpus at Troas when you come— and the books, especially the parchments."*

3. **Financial Support** — Pledging financial support for those who are on the mission field.
   2 Corinthians 9:7 NKJV: *"So let each one give as he purposes in his heart, not grudgingly or of necessity; for God loves a cheerful giver."*

4. **Prayer Support** — Providing a prayer covering before, during, and upon return from the mission field.
   Colossians 4:2–4 NKJV: *"Continue earnestly in prayer, being vigilant in it with thanksgiving; meanwhile praying also for us, that God would open to us a door for the word, to speak the mystery of Christ, for which I am also in chains, that I may make it manifest, as I ought to speak."*

5. **Communication Support** — Providing updates as to what is happening back home as well as being available to receive telephone

communications during hours that may be different from your own time zone.

Philippians 2:19 NKJV: *"But I trust in the Lord Jesus to send Timothy to you shortly, that I also may be encouraged when I know your state."*

6. **Reentry Support** — Taking time to listen to the experiences of the missionary upon his or her return.

Acts 14:28 NKJV: *"So they stayed there a long time with the disciples."*

Finally, we must keep our minds on God and the vision that He has given us. All believers can participate as senders in any one of the six areas mentioned above. Others will actually go, in obedience to the call placed within their hearts. But we all have an important part to play in fulfilling the Great Commission.

If you are a missionary, go—don't allow your circumstances to stop the vision that God has placed in your heart. If you're not a missionary, consider serving as a sender. Ask God for an area in which you can help those who are called to serve on the mission field. But do your part—whatever it is.

The Bible says, *"Then the disciples, each according to his ability, determined to send relief to the brethren dwelling in Judea"* (Acts 11:29 NKJV). We must each have a clear purpose in our hearts and minds as to what God has called us to do, and then we must do it. God will bless both those who go and those who give provision for the vision.

Chapter 9

Global Outreach

*How then shall they call on him in whom they
have not believed? and how shall they believe
in him of whom they have not heard? and how
shall they hear without a preacher? And how
shall they preach, except they be sent?"*
— Romans 10:14–15

"*A***nd you will be my witnesses in Jerusalem,
and in all Judea and Samaria, and to the
ends of the earth"** (Acts 1:8). Serving as a witness
for Christ should be a part of every believer's life.
However, many Christians get nervous when they
hear that the director of evangelism would like to meet
with everyone in preparation for street witnessing. A
fear comes over them because they envision themselves forced into "cold calling" or door-to-door
witnessing throughout neighborhoods.

What is even more terrifying to some Christians is hearing missionaries ask for volunteers to go on a short-term mission trip. Suddenly their imaginations begin to run wild with thoughts of lions, cheetahs, and orangutans chasing them through the jungle in some remote location of Africa!

The Bible says in 2 Timothy 1:7, *"For God has not given us a spirit of fear, but of power and of love and of a sound mind."* It's true that some Christians do possess an actual gift of evangelism, and other Christians have a call for global outreach in the mission field. However, all of us are called to be witnesses for Christ, which should be an extension of our everyday lives. Whether we are chosen by God for global outreach or local evangelism, God will equip us spiritually, physically, and mentally to serve in the field that He has called us to work and there is nothing that we should fear.

God's mandate for Christians is to take the gospel to every tribe, tongue, and nation. To understand this mandate, we must see the world through the eyes of Christ and understand God's love and compassion for all people. His love for people is so great that He gave His only begotten Son for us. If you meditate on that thought alone, you will begin to realize the extent of God's love.

When God called us to go to all nations, He was telling us to think globally. God does not want anyone to miss out on the love and compassion that He has for all humanity; this is why He called us to go to the world. This is why we must think globally, this is why we must plan and communicate globally, and this is why we must see the world from a global perspective when reaching out to the lost.

Since God's mandate for the body of Christ is to reach out globally, it is important to have some understanding of global outreach. Global outreach refers to taking the gospel beyond our immediate sphere of influence. The only way that we can successfully accomplish this task is by having a strategic plan. In other words, for global outreach to be effective, we must have a strategy that involves the entire body of Christ reaching out to the lost.

Strategy

When we think of someone having a global strategy, the first thought that comes to mind is the military. In the military, strategy refers to maneuvering troops into position before the enemy is actually engaged. It's a plan of action. Once the enemy has been engaged, attention shifts to tactics, which refers to the specific actions to defeat the enemy.

The United States military was organized with a global plan in mind. For example, anytime our military forces encounter an opposing enemy, they use both strategy and tactics, based on the size and capability of the threat. Each one of the military branches that represent our armed forces has a specific role in the global plan. Whether it's the U.S. Army, Air Force, Navy, Marine Corps, or Coast Guard, each has its own mission, but all must work together in order to effectively combat an enemy threat. In fact, joint training exercises, in addition to military members serving in joint duty positions, have given our military members a better understanding of how the armed forces work together to accomplish their mission. Training together as a joint force has increased the effectiveness of our armed forces and has given the U.S. military a reputation of being the most powerful military force in the world.

As Christians, we too are members of the most powerful force in the world. We belong to the army of the Lord. We have a duty, an obligation, and a mandate to defeat the enemy and subdue him under the feet of Jesus. For us to succeed, we must strategically position ourselves to win souls for Christ. In doing so, we must know who we are in Christ, the weapons of warfare to defeat the enemy, and the capabilities of the enemy. All too often, however, Christians give reading the Word, praying, and fasting a low priority and then wonder why the gospel isn't being preached around the world and why souls aren't being won to Christ.

Christians not knowing who they are in Christ reminds me of a quote written by a Chinese military strategist by the name of Sun Tzu. In the book *The Art of War*, he says, "If you know the enemy and know yourself, you need not fear the result of a hundred battles. If you know yourself but not the enemy, for every victory gained you will also suffer a defeat. If you know neither the enemy nor yourself, you will succumb in every battle."[23] Christians must realize that they are at war. The enemy is a strategist and a tactician. He has been at this for thousands of years. But our instructions from God are clear—

we are to pursue, overtake, and recover all that the enemy has stolen. We are to do as David did when he and his men came home to Ziklag. As stated in 1 Samuel 30:1-31, we are to engage the enemy, to free the captives and get back what the enemy has stolen. We are to *recover all.*

Many of us are quickly satisfied when we get just a little back of what the devil stole. We begin celebrating and then get lax in our quest for *total* victory. As we do this, we fail to realize that the devil doesn't care whether we go beyond the mark or come short of the mark as long as we miss the mark and as long as we fail to do what God truly planned for our lives. Will the enemy give up territory? Yes, the enemy will give up some territory if it means that we will not have total victory in Christ. This is why we must do as Paul described in Philippians 3:14, we must *"press toward the mark for the prize of the high calling of God in Christ Jesus."* We must not let anything or anyone stop us from accomplishing the plans and goals that God has for each one of us. We must never surrender until we have everything God promised, and we must press forward regardless of the situations that we face!

Satan is fighting every day to win every soul on this earth, and we can't just sit idle, allowing him to rob people of a better life on earth as well as eternal life through Christ Jesus. If we do nothing to reach out to the lost, Satan *will not be like* a roaring lion, but he *will be* a roaring lion, devouring everything in his path. God has given us the authority and power to defeat Satan; now we must do it.

The Bible tells us that *"the thief does not come except to steal, and to kill, and to destroy"* (John 10:10 NKJV). Satan's goal is to steal the Word before it goes forth, to kill the saints before they can share the good news, and to destroy any global outreach plan before it can be implemented. Although the enemy has already been defeated at the cross, we still must know God's plan for our lives, our identity in Christ, and the weapons of warfare that God has given us to win souls for Christ and take the gospel to all nations. It's much like a soldier in an army. After a soldier enlists, he or she is trained in proper authority, instructed in how to fight, and taught everything there is to know about available weapons, but it's up to the soldier to apply this knowledge when confronted in battle. It's the same for us as soldiers in God's army. We cannot allow the thief to rob us. We must use our God-given authority, because we are His children and more than conquerors.

The Bible has already told us who we are and the authority we have in Christ: *"But you belong to God, my dear children. You have already won a victory over those people, because the Spirit who lives in you is greater than the spirit who lives in the world"* (1 John 4:4 NLT). If we do not grasp this clear understanding of who we are in Christ, every enemy appears to be larger and stronger than it really is. Apart from Christ, we can do nothing (John 15:5), and we will surely suffer defeat. But when we place our trust in God and allow Him to work through us, our position against the enemy is strengthened: *"In all these things we are more than conquerors through Him who loved us"* (Romans 8:37). We must, therefore, position ourselves in our calling to defeat the enemy by going into the world to preach the gospel.

When God called us to go into the world, He was saying in effect that we must maneuver ourselves into position, a position where we can use God's weapons and tactics to defeat the enemy. When Christians respond to God's call to go to Africa, Antarctica, Asia, Australia, Europe, North America, or South America, they are positioning themselves to preach the gospel so that poverty can be defeated; hunger wiped out; and depression, oppression, sickness, and disease eliminated. God has called us to go and preach His Word to the unreached people groups of this world so that all will have an opportunity to receive Him as Lord and Savior and acknowledge that He is God!

One Body and One Spirit

In our call to the nations, we *must* be united as one body in Christ, because *"Every kingdom divided against itself is brought to desolation, and a house divided against a house falls"* (Luke 11:17 NKJV). For too long, the body of Christ has been divided by denominations, practices, and beliefs, even though we all read the same Bible. Unless we begin to function as one body and one Spirit, we will continue to waste resources trying to accomplish the mandate that God has directed to all of us.

It's like what you see in driving to work. Hundreds of cars are on the road going in the same direction, but most of the vehicles have only one person in them. However, when fuel prices skyrocket, many people cannot afford the higher prices and begin carpooling in an effort to save money. But it generally takes something drastic to happen before an action is taken.

The Church is doing the same thing. We are going in the same direction, but not as one body. When we unite as one body and one Spirit with a global strategy, Satan will no longer be able to kill, steal, and destroy God's people. The Bible speaks of this powerful unity in Christ: ***"There is one body and one Spirit, just as you were called in one hope of your calling; one Lord, one faith, one baptism; one God and Father of all, who is above all, and through all, and in you all"*** (Ephesians 4:4–5 NKJV). Too many times Satan has used his tactics to divide the body of Christ so that He can conquer us, but it's time that we recognize his tactics and defeat him with the power and authority we have in Christ.

Let's Work Together

The Church must move past division and separation so that global outreach can become a united effort of the entire body of Christ. God wants His people to work together. As He says in Psalm 50:5, ***"Gather my saints together unto me; those that have made a covenant with me by sacrifice."*** God doesn't place a barrier between Christians, but Satan does.

Satan tries his best to divide the body of Christ, but as we come to recognize this evil tactic, we must use the authority and power given to us through Christ by praying, fasting, and taking action to remove division.

Many of us grew up seeing a divided church, and we accepted it as the norm. But when division personally affects you, you tend to think a little differently. I realized this when I once tried to go on a mission trip to Africa with another church. The church required that I fill out an online application. As I began to fill out their online form, I came to a question that asked if I was a member of their particular denomination. Since my wife and I belong to a nondenominational church, I answered no. After I typed my answer, I then submitted the completed questionnaire. A second after I submitted the questionnaire, a screen popped up stating that my application was declined because I did not belong to that particular denomination. What a sad commentary of Christ's body here on earth!

There are over two billion people who have not heard the gospel; you would think that the priority to send missionaries to them would be far more important than the denomination to which someone belongs. Unfortunately, this isn't the case in many churches. This is why it is imperative that the body of Christ come together as one body and in one Spirit so that more people will have an opportunity to hear the gospel.

What's Next?

When the body of Christ begins to work together with a *global* purpose in mind, many more options become available for Christians to serve with a global-outreach team. There are short-term missions that can last from a week to more than a month, medium-term missions that can last from three months to a year, and long-term missions that can last a year or longer. There are also many types of missions that can be organized for global outreach. For example, there are medical assistance missions, literacy and feeding programs, construction missions, humanitarian and crisis-relief missions, economic empowerment, and church-planting/apostolic impartation missions. Serving on a mission team not only enables Christians to help people help themselves, but it can also result in leading others to Christ.

For some Christians who want to get involved in a local foreign community while participating on a long-term mission, tent-making may be a viable option. Tent-making is a term used in missions that describes the Apostle Paul's strategy of financially supporting himself by integrating work and cross-cultural evangelism. Tent-makers work one step at a time to reach local people, sharing the gospel and using their job as a base to establish relationships in the local community.

Finally, training in a variety of different subjects is important for effective global outreach on the mission field. By participating in a formal training program, a person can gain greater insight into apostolic missions. A hands-on approach can provide twenty-first-century strategies for both global and local outreach.

There are many such schools that offer training for global outreach. For example, Master's Touch Ministries Global is part of a vision given to Dr. Patricia Bailey-Jones and her husband, attorney D. Jones, and is an excellent school providing both hands-on and online training to raise up and equip ambassadors for the kingdom of God. If your schedule doesn't allow you to attend a school in your area, there are many books and other online schools with a wealth of knowledge on global outreach.

Where do you go from here: short-term missions, medium-term missions, or long-term missions? You will never know unless you pray, read the Word, and ask God to reveal the answer.

God will speak to you through His Word, but you must position yourself to hear His voice. *"For the word of God is alive and powerful. It is sharper than the sharpest two-edged sword, cutting between soul and spirit, between joint and marrow. It exposes our innermost thoughts and desires"* (Hebrews 4:12 NLT). The Word of God provides the authority and the power to enable you to fulfill Christ's Great Commission to take His gospel to the uttermost parts of the earth.

Conclusion

A window of opportunity is open that has never been open before. Multitudes of lost souls are waiting to hear the message of salvation, and we have the ability to go forth to reap that vast harvest. Lost souls are searching for *peace* that only God can give regardless of whether it's in the United States, Zimbabwe, Colombia, China, Russia, India, Haiti, or some other country. Regardless of the state, city, town, or neighborhood, lost souls are searching for peace. The Great Commission is the means by which unbelievers can be led to Christ to receive the peace that only God can give through salvation. This is why we must go into the world to preach the gospel.

Even though winning lost souls to Christ can be a step-by-step process that can sometimes seem to take an eternity, God uses people to draw other people to Him, and He uses our gifts as part of the process to move us toward our destiny in God. Regardless of our individual role, however, we all have a part to play in winning the lost. In 1 Corinthians 3:5–9, the Bible says, ***"I planted, Apollos watered, but God*** *gave the increase. So then neither he who plants is anything, nor he who waters, but God who gives the increase. Now he who plants and he who waters are one, and each one will receive his own reward according to his own labor. For we are God's fellow workers; you are God's field."*

Jesse Duplantis wrote in his book *The Everyday Visionary,* "This life can be compared to the longest-running play in history. The scenes change and the people change, but each act continues to unfold as we move toward the final curtain in God's plan for man. Some people move toward their destiny in God, others move away from their destiny in God, but still, this story goes on and on. If we choose to accept our destiny, if we choose to conform to the image of Christ Jesus, then we become the characters that God has hand-selected for this generation."[23]

The Church as well as all believers must be engaged in the business of carrying out the Great Commission by both witnessing where we are and by strategically reaching out into all the world. We must realize the value that God has placed on souls. We dare not pass them by; we must *go* and reach out to them.

The Bible says in John 3:16 that *"God so loved the world that He gave His only begotten Son."* If God gave His Son for us, sacrificing Him on the cross of Calvary, how much more must we be willing to give our lives to *reaching people and touching lives around the world.*

Notes

1. U.S. Census Bureau (world population data), viewed at
http://www.census.gov/Press-Release/www/releases/archives/population/012112.html (accessed September 5,2008).

2. David Barrett, *World Christian Encyclopedia: A Comparative Survey of Churches and Religions—AD 30 to 2200,* viewed at
http://www.religioustolerance.org/worldrel.htm (accessed September 5, 2008).

3. Ralph Winter and Bruce Koch, "Finishing the Task," viewed at
http://www.missionfrontiers.org/newslinks/finishing.htm (accessed September 5, 2008).

4. Merriam-Webster's Online Dictionary 2008, viewed at
http://www.merriam-webster.com/dictionary/authority (accessed September 24, 2008).

5. Merriam-Webster's Online Dictionary 2008, viewed at

http://www.merriam-webster.com/dictionary/go (accessed September 5, 2008).

6. The Encarta World English Dictionary, North American Edition, 2008, viewed at http://encarta.msn.com/dictionary_/paradigm.html (accessed September 5, 2008).

7. Brent L. Myers, "Where Are the Poor and Lost?" viewed at http://www.joshuaproject.net/10-40-window.php (accessed September 5, 2008).

8. Patricia Bailey, *Our Unclaimed Inheritance: The Hidden World of African-Americans in Missions* (Palos Verdes: MTM Global Publishing, 2001), 7.

9. Merriam-Webster's Online Dictionary 2008, viewed at http://www.merriam-webster.com/dictionary/vision (accessed September 5, 2008).

10. World Health Organization Mortality Fact Sheet, viewed at http://who.int/globalatlas/dataQuery/reportData.asp?rptType=1 (accessed September 7, 2008).

11. International Bulletin of Missionary Research, dated January 2008, viewed at http://www.internationalbulletin.org/IBMR%20Contents.htm (accessed September 5, 2008).

12. UNICEF Statistics, viewed at http://www.childinfo.org/mortality_challenge.html (accessed September 7, 2008).

13. Numbers of Physicians and Dentists, viewed at http://who.int/globalatlas/dataQuery/reportData.asp?rptType=1 (accessed September 7, 2008).

14. E. M. Bounds, *The Essentials of Prayer* (Kensington: Whitaker House, 1994), 373.

15. Ibid., 374.

16. Merriam-Webster's Online Dictionary 2008, viewed at http://www.merriamwebster.com/dictionary/compassion (accessed September 24, 2008).

17. Shirley Ferguson, *No Longer Bound—Freedom in Christ from the Snares of Satan* (Orlando, FL: Xulon Press, 2008), 22.

18. Belinda Bush, *A Lifestyle of Excellence* (Orlando, FL: Xulon Press, 2008), 24–26.

19. Bill Winston, *Seeding for the Billion Flow* (United States of America, 2007), 28.

20. Bankole Akinmola, *Heirs of the Kingdom* (Atlanta: His Image Marketing Consultants, 1998), 5.

21. Neal Pirolo, *Serving As Senders* (San Diego: Emmaus Rd. Int'l., 1991), 22.

22. Sun Tzu translated by Lionel Giles, edited by James H. Ford, *The Art of War by Sun Tzu—Special Edition* (El Paso: Norte Press, 2005), chapter 3. http://en.wikipedia.org/wiki/The_Art_of_War#The_13_chapters (accessed September 7, 2008).

23. Jesse Duplantis, *The Everyday Visionary* (New York, NY: Touchstone/Howard Books, 2008), 203.

Prayer for the Nations

Father, I thank you that nothing is too big for You. Nothing can compare with Your power and wisdom.

Today I lift my voice to You, that You would be exalted in all the nations. I pray that the leaders of all nations would honor and exalt Your Name, and that Your righteousness would be manifested throughout the world.

In Jesus' Name we stand against the powers of darkness. Nothing, absolutely nothing, can stand against You Oh God, for You are mighty to deliver Your people.

Our prayer oh Lord is that You would indeed make haste to deliver, and shine upon this earth with Your glory. In Jesus' Name. Amen!

Prayer for More Laborers

In Matthew 9:37-38, Jesus says, "The harvest is truly plentiful, but the laborers are few. Therefore pray the Lord of the harvest to send out laborers into His harvest."

The Lord Jesus Christ teaches us to plead with God to call, equip, and send laborers into the harvest. The nations must hear the gospel. Yet, this can happen only as people go out and proclaim the gospel to the nations. It is our responsibility then to pray for laborers who will do this.

The following prayers can help you follow Jesus' command to pray for laborers. You can use these prayers to pray for God to raise a generation of laborers who will evangelize the world. You can also use these prayers to pray for God to call and send laborers into a particular country or people group.

Father, in the name of Jesus, I plead that You will raise up believers who have a heart for church planting. I ask You to call and equip believers who have the skills and determination to plant godly, growing churches (Acts 13:1-3, 26-28).

Lord, I ask You to raise up evangelists who can preach the gospel powerfully and clearly on the mission fields around the world. Mold and shape evangelists who can communicate the gospel to all the cultures of the world (Acts 6:10).

God, I pray that You will raise up believers with the gift of teaching. I plead that they will be sent into all the nations to teach believers the Word of God and how to put into practice its teachings (Ezra 7:10).

I ask You, the Lord of the harvest, to raise up believers who will have a burden about and a call to translating the Bible into the languages of the peoples of the world. Call and equip believers so that the nations can read and hear Your Word (2 Timothy 3:16-17).

Father, I pray that You will call and equip believers who are trained in medicine, agriculture, and business. Let them enter the nations of the world, minister to their needs, and share the gospel with them (Matthew 20:28).

Lord God, I plead that You will burden and convict students and educators about surrendering their lives to Your call to missions (Proverbs 3:5-7). I pray that You will:

— Enable them to have a deep and intimate relationship with Christ;
— Mold them into powerful witnesses for Jesus Christ;
— Grant them spouses that have a clear and definite call to missions;
— Train them to work on the mission field.

—Remove anything that would hinder their service for Jesus Christ.

Father, I ask that You will convict churches about missions and that You will give them a burden for missions. I pray that they will have a "Great Commission Church" that is conducive to people being called to the mission field (Matthew 28:19-20).

Lord, I pray that You would enable Christian groups in other cultures and nations to develop and send missionaries to their own people in both their native land and around the world (Acts 21:37-22:21).

Father, I pray that You will burden believers to be involved in all facets of missions. Give Your people a heart to support missions. Burden them and move them to be involved in mission trips (Matthew 28:19-20).

Father, I ask that You would bless the groups and organizations in the churches that encourage and teach people about missions. Bless their labors. Give them fresh and relevant ideas to motivate believers to be on mission. Cause the young people who come through these groups or organizations develop a consuming passion for missions (Acts 13:1-3).

God, You are the Creator and owner of all things. All the money in the world is Yours. I pray that You would cause money to flow into the missions agencies and organizations of Christianity. Move upon the hearts and the minds of people to give generously, joyously, and sacrificially to the cause of the gospel across the world (Proverbs 21:1).

Father, I ask You to raise up churches that will have a burden to pray for the harvesting of the nations. Mold and shape churches so that they will be houses of prayer for the nations. Grant them an unceasing burden to pray for missionaries and the nations of the world. Give them insight and understanding how to seek You for the fulfillment of the Great Commission (Matthew 28:19-20).

In Jesus' Name. Amen!

Prayer for Salvation

Dear Heavenly Father, I come to You in the Name of Jesus. You said in Your Word that whosoever shall call upon the name of the Lord shall be saved. (Romans 10:13).

Father, I am calling on Jesus right now. I believe He died on the cross for my sins, that He was raised from the dead on the third day, and He's alive right now.

Lord Jesus, I am asking You now, come into my heart. Live Your life in me and through me.

I repent of my sins and surrender myself totally and completely to You.

Heavenly Father, by faith I now confess Jesus Christ as my new Lord and from this day forward, I dedicate my life to serving Him.

In Jesus' Name. Amen!

Printed in the United States
213226BV00001B/2/P

9 781607 914051